EMPOWERMENT IN ORGANIZATIONS

How to Spark Exceptional Performance

EMPOWERMENT IN
ORGANIZATIONS ❖
How to Spark Exceptional Performance

Judith F. *Vogt, Ph*.D., & *Kenneth* L. *Murrell,* D.B.A.

8517 Production Avenue
San Diego, California 92121

Copyright © 1990 by University Associates, Inc.
ISBN: 0-88390-238-9
Library of Congress Catalog Card Number 89-21244
Printed in the United States of America

Library of Congress Cataloging-in-Publication Data

Vogt, Judith F.
  Empowerment in organizations : how to spark exceptional
performance / Judith F. Vogt, Kenneth L. Murrell.
    p. cm.
  Includes bibliographical references.
  ISBN 0-88390-238-9
  1. Organizational effectiveness. 2. Organizational change.
3. Job enrichment. 4. Performance. I. Murrell, Kenneth L.
II. Title.
HD58.9.V63 1990
658.3′ 14—dc20   89-21244
                                                          CIP

Jacket Designed by Paul Bond
Interior Designed by Carolyn Ingalls

This book is printed on acid-free, recycled stock that meets
or exceeds the minimum GPO and EPA specifications
for recycled paper.

PREFACE

This book is more than a book about a management concept. It is about who we are, who we are becoming, and how we are getting there. It is about our families, our friends, our colleagues, and our places of work; it is about our students and our professional relationships. It is about our community and our world and our visions for both. Empowerment is central to each of us, but in different ways. For Judy, empowerment is how she sees her life goal: to enable others, to build with them something greater than what we can achieve as individuals. For Ken, empowerment is how he conceptualizes his world. Both of us have incorporated self-directed models of empowerment to guide our own learning and to define the themes of our lives. We may not always "do it right," but, holding empowerment as an achievable ideal, we work hard to be empowered and to empower others.

We are fortunate to live and work with others who allow us to be empowered and who value empowerment. We take this opportunity to recognize Karen and David and Cathy and Kenyan as well as Terry, Diana (DP), and Katherine for their support and contributions to this effort. They have firsthand knowledge of the rewards — and pains — associated with "empowering us" during the thinking and writing stages of the book. We are grateful to our colleagues at the University of West Florida and The Florida State University for their interest, questions, and suggestions. In addition, we thank Carol Nolde, Roberta Clark, and Carolyn Ingalls for their dedication and perseverance on our behalf. Finally, we recognize all of the leaders, managers, and employees from whom we have learned so much about empowering others in organizations.

As you read this book think first about yourself. Consider your past — the personal images, events, and memories you can use to build a life description for yourself based on empowerment. Then think about your family and friends — your own personal support network — as you explore the idea of participating in empowering relationships. Next look at your work group and think about how it is or can become empowering and empowered. Think of the systems and societies you know of that are empowered and develop an understanding of the relationships between self and society they contain. Finally, create for yourself a reality and a vision that let you grasp the potential for empowerment in your present and future life.

This book and the process of writing it have strengthened our friendship and our respect for each other while empowering us as individuals and as a team. We hope the book will lend you support as you explore the turns and corners and depths and heights of empowerment — for yourself and your organization.

Judith F. Vogt
Kenneth L. Murrell

CONTENTS

INTRODUCTION — THE EMPOWERMENT CHOICE: HISTORY, FRAMEWORK, AND VISIONS

 Overview

Chapter 1 examines today's world as the setting of a new conceptual framework for managing and facilitating human development. It looks at the groundswell of demand for recognition, involvement, and a sense of worth by both individuals and organizations and offers a new construct for the future — that of empowerment. The authors begin by examining the inadequacy of the motivational thought of the early postwar period while recognizing its usefulness as a foundation for the emerging concept of empowerment. Empowerment is then defined and the central themes and format of the book are presented.

The empowering of individuals, groups, organizations, and societies is a noble, necessary, and natural part of human development. In some cases empowerment occurs without our awareness of the events and processes that induce it. In today's global society, for example, pressures for empowerment are growing. People in Burma, Poland, South Africa, Armenia, Afghanistan, Korea, Nicaragua, and elsewhere are asserting their demand to be recognized, valued, and consulted. Their insistence is causing enormous turmoil and shaking political and economic power structures. Government officials feel threatened and insecure, often because they do not understand the new demands. In the past, governments designed the structure within which people were to act in ways the leadership believed were right and necessary; then they sought to protect that structure from destabilizing influences arising from the people. In the last fifty years, however, with the advent of mass communications and the spread of human rights ideals, a new orientation has emerged; more people are not only demanding a voice but also demonstrating their ability to manage their own lives and participate in the decision making and developmental processes of their nations and organizations.

In the United States as well, workers are demonstrating their desire to be directly involved and, more importantly, to show their ability to make a difference to their organizations' growth and development. Many own their businesses through profit-sharing or employee-ownership programs; others offer workable suggestions that provide significant savings in operational costs. And, just as government officials feel threatened and are uncertain about how to proceed in the face of these new realities, so too do the leaders of American businesses, industries, and organizations.

They — and all of us — need a new conceptual framework, a new way to look at relationships among people, be they citizens of countries or employees and managers of corporations. In this book we offer such a framework, the *empowerment choice*. In the remainder of this chapter we look at the history of empowerment and provide a preliminary definition. In the following chapters we further refine the concept of empowerment and discuss how it can be applied to America's organizations.

Recent developments in the wider society have helped to "raise up" the idea of empowerment and have prompted major changes in American culture. New social relationships such as the emergence of women as active and equal participants, increased volunteerism, changes in family structure and membership, and altered teaching/learning relationships in elementary through college classrooms have widened the group of active participants and signaled a search for communal values. New information technologies and the rapid increase of information sharing, assisted by the personal computer (PC) revolution, have brought our legal, political, and medical fields under intense scrutiny. Some social commentators have also seen a new emphasis on the spirituality of life. These developments have led to a society that sees itself differently and acts differently; they have altered the values, norms, and attitudes we bring to our daily lives and to our nation's relationships with other nations. And they have combined to influence the shape and management of our organizations.

A THEORETICAL FRAMEWORK: FROM MOTIVATION TO EMPOWERMENT

For more than fifty years, we Americans have focused attempts to renew and reorganize the work world on the self. We have studied the behavior and motivation of the individual in numerous organizational contexts — from businesses, volunteer groups, and churches to the family. The American cultural environment, with its tradition of philosophical individualism, was supportive of such an explosion of theory and research about individual motivation. (See Figure 1.)

World War II, which broke down limiting role expectations for certain groups (e.g., workers, women, blacks) set the stage for a re-examination of the *person* and his or her uniqueness. Psychologists like Henry Murray, Karen Horney, Abraham Maslow, Carl Rogers, Eric Fromm, Kurt Lewin, and David McClelland, among many others, initiated the contemporary emphasis on the self. Educational and organizational psychologists and practitioners then took over from the clinical and social psychologists, beginning the challenging task of conceptualizing and applying the new understanding of individual psychology to organizational settings. The most significant focus of the 1950s and early 1960s was on the concept of *motivation,* which gave researchers and employers a handle on how to utilize the new views of human psychology in learning and work situations. Douglas McGregor's book *The Human Side of Enterprise* (1960) provides a focal point for this transition. By the late 1960s and early 1970s the human potential perspective and its orientation toward individual growth were well entrenched in our schools and work places. The study of motivation and the focus on the

FIGURE 1.   Motivation to Empowerment

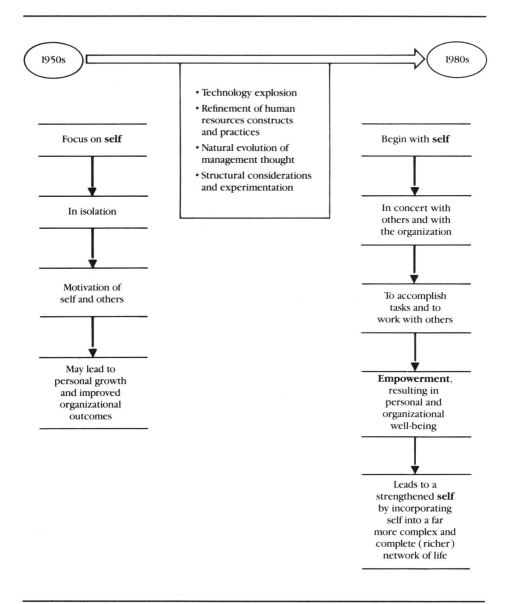

individual's needs, wants, potential, and growth were made the foundation of major organizational changes.

Since the early 1970s, however, additional factors — some a natural evolution of this trend and others stemming from unrelated developments — have affected American work life. The current explosion of technology and innovations in management thinking have forced managers to take into account far more variables: human resource concepts have been refined; organizational structures are no longer considered unalterable; and, most importantly, people have learned that they can have more high-quality and personally fulfilling experiences by working together. Along with the crises discussed in Chapter 2 and the nine trends for the 1990s examined in the concluding chapter, these changes point clearly to the need for a new rallying point.

The construct of empowerment is emerging as that new force in organizational life. Like the postwar emphasis on motivation, empowerment starts with the self; but it does not stop there. Empowerment realizes and reconceptualizes the relationship among tasks, work, achievements, and connectedness. The last fifty years have not only enriched the individual, incorporating him or her into a far more complex and complete network of life; they have also helped us come to terms with our heritage of community. As a nation we have come to this point in our history because of our experiences of working together while continuing to value ourselves as individuals. Daniel Yankelovich (1981) has called this progression a movement toward an ethic of commitment. Recent efforts to apply the concept of empowerment recognize this ethical aspect of all systems of interrelatedness.

Understanding the historical development from motivational theory to the concept of empowerment can provide managers and leaders the framework they need to react positively rather than defensively to the new realities. Whereas the motivational orientation seemed to ask "What can we do *to* employees so they will contribute in the ways we see as most useful?," an empowerment orientation asks "What can we do to facilitate people's individual and joint contributions to their own and to the organization's well-being?" The motivation question comes from a posture of control and implies no necessary commitment to personal or group development. The empowerment question, on the other hand, recognizes the role responsibility of leaders and managers but does not intimate control. Instead, it sets out a commitment to make both personal development and organization development opportunities of the process. Empowerment, based on liberating and not controlling human energy, demands major shifts in organizational structures to make them reflect the sort of power that enables each person to be all he or she can.

Although the theoretical and operational dimensions of empowerment are different from those of motivation, motivation has played a significant role in the emergence of empowerment. Along with theories of personality and growth of the self, it has helped us understand how an individual attains a firm sense of worthiness and well-being. It has moved us toward our next enabling human construct — *empowerment.*

TODAY'S ORGANIZATIONS AND EMPOWERMENT

Running through the research literature on organizational behavior and through the operations of many successful organizations "is a common theme which emphasizes the power of confident people, passionately committed to meaningful goals, acting in accordance with their own higher values, taking risks and demonstrating initiative and creativity in the service of these goals" (Thomas & Velthouse, 1985, p. 1). In the 1950s and 1960s this theme of individual well-being was embodied in the literature on motivation and self-realization (e.g., Maslow, Rogers) and in a humanistic model of existence. Today (and probably for the near future), this theme of individual well-being is being expressed in terms of empowerment. Empowerment models have incorporated research findings on such subjects as the individual's search for identity, cognitive styles, leadership, and organizational structure.

Empowerment today is still in an embryonic stage; much of what exists is theoretical and has not been empirically confirmed. Moreover, there are, at best, only inadequate definitions of empowerment. Even in this early state, however, empowerment is having a significant impact on managerial and organizational thought and actions. Consultants like Peter Block (1987) are writing about their experiences with empowerment and recommending it to their clients, and scholars and other management writers are also rethinking the issue of power. Theory and practice are thus emerging simultaneously.

Many organizations are already implementing strategies, activities, and perspectives based on empowerment assumptions. Scott Paper Company's National Resources Division (NRD) November 1985 newsletter explains the corporate vision in terms of human resource excellence, which means to "continue to build a culture that will attract and develop people with superior capabilities and to enable them to achieve outstanding results." For Rich Fluri (1985), NRD's human resources director, "empowerment means providing employees with the environment, proper tools, and resources that enable them to contribute at a higher level, and for management to help them achieve these goals by coaching, teaching and enabling." Xerox (Kanter, 1983) defines the concept of job enrichment as increasing responsibility, individual discretion, and autonomous decision making. Wilbert Gore, founder of Gore and Associates, Inc. (Gore-Tex), has advocated empowerment since 1958. The following statement is typical of his sales and marketing literature: "We have to release the creativity and potential of human beings. The way that you do this is to give people the maximum amount of freedom."

John Naisbitt (1984) sees the United States as heading into a severe labor shortage, with intensified competition for employees at all organizational levels. People entering the work force will have the choice of working for a hierarchically dominated, authoritarian corporation or a corporation that is implementing new, open, organic, and democratic models.

A major purpose of the following chapters, therefore, is to help readers become more informed about the emerging work place so that they can make intelligent future choices for themselves as well as for their organizations. A second purpose is to prepare them for what they will encounter in empowering organizations and in organizations beginning to institute empowerment. Knowing about empowerment will provide them a basis for assessing their own successes; weaknesses; and, most importantly, their personal reactions to an empowering environment.

In summary, a look at what has brought individuals and organizations to this point reveals three stages. In the first stage demand for a new orientation was created through changes in numerous social, economic, and political facets of life. In the second stage organizational leaders recognized the need to respond to the new cultural realities rather than to maintain the status quo. Finally, in the last stage, they realized that the incorporation of empowerment was congruent with the process and dimensions of an emerging American society characterized by principles of shared responsibility and commitment.

WHAT IS EMPOWERMENT?

In simple definitional terms, the verb to *empower* means to *enable,* to *allow* or to *permit* and can be conceived as both self-initiated and initiated by others. For social change agents, empowering is an act of building, developing, and increasing power through cooperation, sharing, and working together. It is an interactive process based on a synergistic, not a zero-sum, assumption about power; that is, the process of empowerment enlarges the power in the situation as opposed to merely redistributing it.

Empowerment starts as a pragmatic approach to rethinking power in terms of what *can be* rather than what *has been.* This can be illustrated by thinking about several myths derived from our belief in rugged individualism, the industrial revolution, and the laws of natural science. One myth is that strong individuals achieved such feats as conquering the Western frontier totally on their own. Today we know that the wilderness hero was supported by a family and by a community of neighbors. Another myth is that social organizations can control human resources in the same manner as they do physical resources. At first, this belief seemed appropriate. Later, unions began organizing, and government started intervening. An increasingly educated (and empowered) work force began to react to the power of owners and managers. A final fallacy is the assumption that no power can be created or used without losing other power, a sort of social first law of thermodynamics. Yet social power and human energy defy the laws of physics, at least the laws prior to the concept of relativity. We cannot automatically apply physical laws in the social domain without undermining our understanding of social power.

The new principles of empowerment do not rest on past traditions and myths about human behavior nor on Newtonian physics. The human species is capable of modifying its behavior, as well as its organizations and social systems whenever survival demands it. Cultural differences alone show how many optional models are available. Japanese culture is currently showing us some of the many different ways we can go about organizing work. Such lessons from outside our own culture can lead us to re-examine our own beliefs and take advantage of the adaptability of the human species.

One of the professional specialties concerned with helping organizations alter their cultures is organization development (OD). The OD approach builds on the premise that human, and thus organizational, behavior can change and that such change can simultaneously improve output measures (profit) as well as empower individual members of the organization. Professionals in OD have demonstrated that organizations and their leaders not only can create power for the good of more than just a limited few; they also can have a profound impact on the work cultures and leadership styles in these organizations.

Whereas most experts define power as A's ability to control or change B's behavior, the concept of empowerment implies that A can influence or affect B so that A and B's interaction produces more power or influence for both of them. In fact, A ... n (all actors engaged in working together) have the potential to empower one another, so that the net result is an increase in power for all involved, not just a new equilibrium of power through distribution. A's influence over B is replaced by thinking in terms of empowerment as power $(A + B + \ldots n)$ enhanced or increased through cooperation and sharing. The result represents increases in social goods or net positive social gain. Although the notions of social goods or net positive social gain are relative, the result of an A ... n empowerment is that recipients view the result as beneficial. Any organizational action can illustrate successful empowerment if the social system is able to accomplish more than it did prior to the empowerment and if its members value this action and its consequences.

As the world moves beyond the postindustrial era, our notions of power will again be forced to change. These changes will probably occur first in work organizations facing increased competition from abroad and later at the societal or nation-state level. Perhaps in two to three more generations, our assumptions about power and competition in the work place and in society will be quite different, as the culture shifts from material concerns to broader issues about the quality of life, the spirituality of existence, and human relationships.

Many progressive organizations have already implemented programs to enhance the quality of their employees' work lives. Yet before the principle of empowerment can be added to this concern, other changes will have to occur. An empowerment culture will need to take advantage of the competitive energy that is a central force in our society, using it as one way to help actors A and B produce more than either A or B can achieve alone. The competitive struggle can be empowering, however, only as long as the end result is social growth and organizational, not individual, gain. Since America's earliest days, its competitive dynamism has been a national hallmark. Now, as some have begun to question this dynamism, the notion of empowerment can serve to re-energize our collective spirit and focus our attention on outperforming our global competitors while looking for better ways to live together.

As we search for these new ways, we need to remind ourselves that empowerment is not merely an outcome but a process with its roots in the changing social, economic, and political structures of society. It is a way of being, a way of thinking — not merely a fad, tactic, or a quick fix. Empowerment, a personal, life-long process that requires fundamental changes, can be built only gradually. Each step must be solidly constructed, starting from the self; the individual must be self-confident, competent, and clear about the process of empowerment. Once the self is ready, the process can move on to relationships, groups, organizations, nations, and society as a whole.

ABOUT THIS BOOK

This book is primarily intended for middle- and upper-level managers, organizational leaders, and professionals in organization development (OD), human resource development (HRD), and training and development (T & D). It is meant to empower its readers, as well as to open doors leading to empowerment. In attempting to integrate macro and global perspectives with micro and concrete strategies, it offers the practitioner both a broad framework for understanding empowerment and the practical advice necessary to apply it to a particular system.

Chapter 2, "The Opportunity of Crises: Empowerment" explores the global perspective in terms of six contemporary crises that point to the need for a new vision. Chapter 3, "Leadership for Empowerment," examines the managerial responsibilities, skills, and roles necessary in initiating empowerment. Chapter 4, "Foundations of the Concept of Empowerment" describes the social and theoretical antecedents of empowerment and reviews the research findings on motivation, values, leadership, environment, learning theory, organizational structure, system integration, organizational development, and ethics as they relate to the process of instituting empowerment. Chapter 5, "Frameworks for "Empowerment" further refines the author's definition of empowerment and concludes with a process model of empowerment.

Chapter 6, "Pictures of Empowerment," discusses the managerial and organizational characteristics of empowerment. It then explores the creation of energy through application of empowerment and presents the well-functioning group as the primary vehicle for changing systems.

Chapter 7, "Parallel Action Empowerment: From Self to System," describes a parallel change process, the stages of which are congruent for both the individual (self) and the organization (system). The chapter describes this change process and then discusses in depth two categories of empowerment interventions.

Chapter 8, "Empowering Interventions," presents seven principles for applying the empowerment concept and offers a model of planned change especially developed for empowerment; the latter focuses on the individual, the relationships within the organization, and the organization as a whole. The chapter concludes with a discussion of transformation and reviews an orientation emphasizing the interdependence of all levels as a guiding premise for enacting action-empowerment.

Chapter 9, "Enacting Empowerment," offers specific examples of how empowerment might affect individuals, groups, and organizations and how such settings as education, health care, law, government, and business would look if they were empowered. The heart of the chapter recognizes nine trends for the 1990s, which both provide the foundations for empowerment and create an environment demanding personal and organizational action.

Chapter 10, "Empowerment Today and Tomorrow: A Paradigm of Choice," presents a choice between two paradigms of power: the creation and liberation of power within our organizations or the limitation and hierarchical control of power.

Each chapter begins with an overview; many contain models, figures, and lists to draw attention to particular concerns or to supplement the text. An extensive bibliography is provided for the reader who wants to explore specific subjects in greater depth. Finally, Appendix A offers instruments for assessing individuals and systems as they begin to examine and implement empowerment.

CHAPTER 2

THE OPPORTUNITY OF CRISES: EMPOWERMENT

 Overview

Chapter 2 uses an orientation of growth through crisis to consider several contemporary human and social crises that point to the need for a new way of thinking about relationships. It describes six global and personal crises — of energy, confusion, conflict, stress, alienation, and spirituality — and considers the opportunities each one offers to implement empowerment principles.

In a stable, unchanging environment, growth and development are not critical issues. In this world, however, as it approaches the twenty-first century, stability is rare and promises to become even scarcer in the future. Why then do so many organizations focus on maintenance, and why do so many managers look to greater control as the solution to their problems?

One explanation is that so much change is confronting us that our personal, organizational, and even cultural systems are overwhelmed. In 1970 Alvin Toffler described this phenomenon as "future shock." He re-emerged in 1980 with *The Third Wave,* an optimistic tome that explained the problem in a global context. In it Toffler pointed to an overall pattern, or wave, of change and offered ways to predict future waves and the turbulence associated with them.

The authors believe that the crises facing us in these waning years of the twentieth century are opportunities. The viewpoint that crisis presents an opportunity for growth is partly derived from crisis counseling theory, which views crisis states as times when an individual or a family can be helped to make important changes in emotional growth and behavior. Crisis intervention requires the counselor to trust the client's ability to cope with the strain of the process and emerge anew, and he or she must stand ready to provide emotional support while allowing deeper explorations of the self. Such an exploration takes courage and competence to create a new knowledge of our own power.

Similarly, in global, national, and organizational contexts, opportunities of crisis exist for those who see the emerging patterns and can successfully manage the waves of change. The three-pronged power of knowledge Toffler employs — historical hindsight, insight built on introspection, and educated foresight — is available to all. For leaders it is a foundation for empowerment, a prerequisite for actively shaping the future and not just being swept along by it. Such a proactive stance is equally imperative for the individual and for society as a whole. In this chapter the authors examine six of today's and tomorrow's most critical crises, both global and personal, with an emphasis on the opportunities they present and the environmental demands for empowerment they place on our organizations.

THE ENERGY CRISIS

From a global perspective the inevitable depletion of our nonrenewable resources is a reality, even though many individuals and social institutions do not acknowledge or act on this basic certainty. The solution is also clear: the energy needed to drive future economic development and our future tools and toys must come from renewable sources. Yet, although we know these sources exist, we are not responding to the coming crisis in supply in a proactive or timely fashion; our response may well be too little and too late.

Many people see power, like energy, as a finite resource and view power conservation and sharing as particularly illogical acts. Like industrialized countries competing for their share of the world's nonrenewable resources, many individuals believe that "If I don't use power, I'll lose it." This paradigm (world view) of power is well grounded in humanity's thousands of years of competitive struggle for control of finite resources. Only in the present generation have we begun to reconceptualize both power and natural resources as something other than zero-sum realities. Today our most needed resources, energy in particular, could well be renewable if we are willing to work together to make such a possibility a reality.

The energy crisis, therefore, is both a paradigm for old ways of thinking about power and an opportunity to prepare for a future that demands recycling of resources and, more importantly, cooperative development of renewable sources of energy. It seems clear that we can best create new energy and increase global economic development by sharing technologies rather than by competing for scarce resources. New technologies and creative forms of human organizations can be linked to create power.

The personal energy form we call *motivation* is also a renewable resource. Empowering organizations — those environments in which the motivation for commitment, responsibility, and connectedness is encouraged, not limited — can create motivation as an abundant resource. Motivation, in turn, will help create new solutions to our global crises and foster a demand for new forms of shared leadership and decentralized structures, many of which have already begun to emerge. Whereas in the past we assumed that physical energy had to be produced by giant oil refineries and huge nuclear plants, the advent of solar power has allowed us to see the potential of small, dispersed production plants. The solar panel is a good analogy for the empowered employee creating energy (motivation) and networking with others in small, decentralized work groups. Such an analogy not only helps us rethink what power is but also forces us to reconsider our assumptions about motivation and leadership and the form and structure of our future organizations.

An empowerment approach benefits both the individual and the organization; it is a way of being that solves the organization's own energy crisis. Empowerment — like the quest for renewable energy — defines power as generative and not just distributive, as the myth of power has led us to believe.

THE CRISIS OF CONFUSION

In both individuals and society the response to rapid change is frequently uncertainty and confusion about what should be done (the goal) and how best to do it (the means). The resultant ambiguity may result in inaction or paralysis or, as mentioned previously, in a search for stability and greater control. These are common defense mechanisms for both individuals and social systems and will lead eventually to the breakdown of a system that is out of touch with its environment and circumstances. In an organization, both responses prepare fertile ground for growth of a bureaucratic culture, a clear symptom of a problem that goes very deep (Hummel, 1977). Far from reducing the confusion resulting from the accelerated pace and increasing complexity of change, they increase it by closing out needed information, thus entrenching management in the past and denying potential new sources of power — because of the disruptions they might create.

The positive and healthy direction a social system can move toward when faced with an ambiguous environment is easy to explain but challenging to implement. Two questions must be answered once information from the environment is recognized. First, what is there in the situation and in the system itself that is valued as a goal? In essence, what is the vision or purpose of the system? Second, what capabilities (or means) exist within the system to accomplish its purpose? After exploring these fundamental goals and available means, managers will need to identify other goals that have emerged and determine what additional means will be necessary to move the system out of confusion and toward action. In short, what will empower the system to take action? If the answers to these questions rely on the stability/control response, then the system's coping capacities and strategies will be inadequate for the changing environment.

If, however, the ends/means search results in a better strategic positioning of the individual or the organization, then the crisis will have become an opportunity for empowerment. With a clear direction and a grounded sense of reality about what the system has the means to accomplish, management becomes the balancing of sources and forces and the creation of new and more effective responses to environmental turbulence.

Organizations and individuals who know what they want, and who know their capacities to achieve it, are powerful. Confusion and lack of direction or purpose create powerlessness and a denial or alteration of reality for the sake of self-protection. Yet a crisis of confusion can create opportunities for change if the individual or system takes the time — and the risks — necessary to deal with it. But any system that meets confusion by simply redoubling efforts in the old direction is not on a path of recovery. Systems that are too busy trying to "stay ahead of the game" often realize too late that the rules of the game have changed and that opportunity has been lost. Empowerment is built on a clear understanding of purpose and methods. For both individuals and organizations, power begins when they determine what they want and how to get it.

THE CRISIS OF CONFLICT

In a world of deeply imbedded interests and stubbornly held convictions we are challenged to discover how such strong-willed and often conflicting purposes can coexist. Nonetheless, if our species is to survive into the next century, or the one after that, better conflict-management skills and more collaborative organizational forms must emerge.

On a global level, as the superpowers begin to negotiate agreements to assure each other's continued existence, other nation-states seem to be following their example — evidence of the power of "modeling" in crisis situations. Recent developments in the Middle East and in southern Africa seem to be following the more peaceful course laid out by the United States and the Soviet Union. It would be historically naive, of course, to assume that these trouble spots will change quickly or permanently, for backsliding is a normal part of the establishment of a new national or international equilibrium.

For individuals and professionals too, the empowerment perspective suggests a new form of the power paradigm that allows more than a zero-sum conclusion to all disputes. At Harvard and other leading law schools, legal scholars are seeking nonadversarial conflict-management strategies. In other areas too, a new orientation toward conflict — one recognizing that conflict resolution need not always be a case of right or wrong, good or bad, win or lose, or survival of the strongest — is gaining credibility. Creative conclusions that uncover win-win options can also be found.

If old frameworks are altered and creative solutions are allowed to come forward, mutual advantage can be gained from directly confronting individual or organizational conflicts. Although certain battlegrounds (e.g., where physical resources are indeed finite) are resistant to change, elsewhere the resource pie can be enlarged or managed more carefully and long-term win-win solutions are possible. Competing divisions within corporations, for example, can develop cooperative strategies for success, and organizations can structure their reward systems to encourage cooperative behavior. We can also use competition to bring out the best in both sides, structuring a situation fairly and acting under mutually agreed-on rules, as in a sports contest.

In the global economy too, joint ventures and other cooperative arrangements have already benefited producers in many countries; few would deny that American automobiles have improved because of Japanese competition. In an open world market, organizations able to respond rapidly with the highest quality will always have a chance; and in a growing global marketplace, with the potential of nearly five billion consumers, all can be empowered. In such a market, however, although short-term rigidities can be overcome, an organization lacking a long-term global strategy may simply not survive. Growth drives economic systems, and the world's needs are increasing at an exponential rate that empowers individual consumers as well as producers. This growth potential demands new ways of managing international conflict through an economic system that benefits from world peace and prosperity. The incentives for economic growth and better conflict management are becoming more and more clear.

The opportunity to create means for consensus formation in international and organizational settings is a major step toward world peace. If global actors continue to experiment with managing conflict, while managers are doing the same at both the personal and organizational levels, a new era of human evolution is possible. The opportunity inherent in the present crisis of conflict may be the chance to lay the issues and concerns of all sides on the table, the first step toward empowerment at all levels of existence — from self to society. This critical step allows us to deal with real data, not the facades and politics of power and control. We can create power, through the development of win-win frameworks, where we could once imagine only win-lose scenarios.

THE CRISIS OF STRESS

This world — with its increasing economic competition; ambiguity; change; constant interaction; and complex, multi-leveled conflicts — has resulted in significantly increased stress for much of the world's population. Moreover, in an organization where empowerment is the norm, stress can be created as unavoidable conflicts rise to the surface and must be confronted. The restructuring of relationships, plus the need to learn different conflict-resolution strategies, can add considerably to stress and require new methods of managing conflict that are difficult in themselves. Even so, for individuals and social systems, a crisis of stress offers an opportunity to create new patterns of social interaction for managing conflict.

At all levels, living in a complex and dynamic world requires strong systems of support. The numerous "anonymous" groups of parents, alcoholics, overeaters, gamblers, and so forth can serve as useful models for organizational leaders seeking to respond to the stress of change. In the helping professions networks have long served to connect and help members. It seems likely that, as new types of leadership develop, supervisors, managers, or other organizational leaders of various industries will forge their own networks of support.

Just as individuals and professionals need a support system of friends and colleagues to help them cope with stress, organizations require coping mechanisms and support systems, especially in periods of growth. Industry associations and, in some cases, governments are supportive allies to organizations. In some countries, governments are seen as the natural and supportive allies of business interests, just as they are the firm supporters of certain other countries (e.g., Great Britain for the United States).

It is important for individuals to design their own support systems and coping mechanisms. In the mid-1970s, the National Institute of Mental Health (NIMH) funded the Youth Self-Advocacy Program (YSA). The purpose of the project was to help children help themselves, not to do things *for* them. In one neighborhood, the young people discussed their desires and needs to be financially more independent, especially if they wanted to go to college or a technical training program or to provide extras for their own children. They also wanted to develop a neighborhood park, buy equipment for it, supervise it, enjoy it, and make it safe for younger children. Over the months, they explored various ways, individually and as a group, to earn money. They designed committees to talk to city officials, local business owners, and neighborhood residents. They started bank accounts — for the park and for themselves — that necessitated convincing bank officials that they could be responsible and that age was not a fair criterion for determining whether people were doing constructive work for the community. The important factor is that *they,* the *youths,* were their own advocates. The YSA facilitators counseled, suggested, educated, and questioned, but the kids planned and carried out the projects. The YSA helpers were empowering; the youth were empowered.

All such proactive responses to a crisis of stress provide not just coping skills, but also an increased capacity to be empowered. Systems, like individuals, must respond to stress in ways that enhance their capacity to handle power; the coping capacity of the individual or the organization is a necessary prerequisite for creating more power in the system and for allowing strategies of empowerment to emerge. As power increases, more and higher levels of performance can be achieved, but such growth can occur only if the coping *and* enhancing capacities are developed. Survival in our fast-changing world requires the development and implementation of these stress-response foundations.

THE CRISIS OF ALIENATION

The most obvious casualty of machine-paced, large organizations is the worker on the assembly line. Studies of this person's alienation are legion. Critics have also noted the prevalence of the alienated, highly conforming clerical manager and staff technician. In fact, few participants in industrial organizations seem to avoid alienated work lives and what sociologists in the 1960s, using Durkheim's term, described as a sense of *anomie.* Now, in this almost postindustrial era (for we are certainly in a major transition), the potential exists to respond more effectively to this crisis of alienation, especially when we recognize the true social costs of such alienation.

In a period when the Federal Government is contemplating a "war on drugs" that could cost taxpayers billions of dollars, we need to ask ourselves why we have a drug problem in the first place. What is so alienating about our society that a sizable proportion of our population is desperate to escape it? What is there in people's everyday reality that makes a life-threatening escape with drugs so appealing? What leads people to so deny their own worth and capabilities that they cover them up in a chemical fog?

Research conducted several years ago by David McClelland (1971) found a correlation between escaping with drugs and alcohol and an unsatisfied power drive. The power motive, when it had little chance of being met in a person's social or work life, apparently sought outlet in the fantasy world of an alcohol or drug euphoria. Both alcoholics and drug addicts seemed well aware of the risks to health and life they traded for a temporary feeling of being powerful and in control. This research fits well with a common pattern of work alienation in which an employee compensates for a boring job with a drug-induced fantasy of power shared with a community of others engaging in similar behavior.

Many children of the 1970s and 1980s have had ample opportunity to observe abuse of drugs, alcohol, and food in an alienated family setting. Their coping patterns of escapism are frequently reinforced by an equally alienating school system that holds students' power potential in constant check while seeming to demand obedience and conformity at all costs. Of course, social problems as serious as drug abuse have their roots in more than one aspect of society; indeed we can identify alienating environments in virtually all of our social institutions, including hospitals and churches as well as schools and work sites.

The issue of alienation and substance abuse has come so strongly to our attention primarily because we place a high valuation on people in the public limelight. The death of Bill Buntin (a professional basketball player in the 1970s) was but a quiet omen of what has come in the 1980s; such luminaries as Lawrence Taylor (professional football player), Len Bias (University of Maryland basketball player), John Belushi (entertainer), Betty Ford (former First Lady), Bruce Kimball (Olympic diver), and literally hundreds of others have made headlines because of their addictions, deaths, or crimes against others. These people, who are presumably fulfilled and "doing what they do best," are apparently still searching.

Most substance abusers report that they are unable to connect with others. Taylor, who was twice suspended from the New York Giants football team, was recognized as perhaps the best linebacker ever. Nonetheless, during a 1988 news conference he said, "I know all about the dangers drinking and driving bring other people. But . . . if I don't care what happens to me now, can I really think about what might happen to others?" Much of today's alienation runs very deep; it is a distancing not only from others but also from the self. And it is not simply involved with the conflicts of "doing a good job." It also reflects our personal relationships and the way we work together.

The opportunity arising from the pervasive alienation of our culture can best be seen in the increasing number of self-help groups and substance-abuse treatment centers. Addicts (the most fortunate ones) are being offered treatment options in for-profit institutions and in numerous employer-sponsored employee assistance programs. The success of Alcoholics Anonymous and similar groups suggests that a person who enters a self-help program, either voluntarily or motivated by threatened loss of job or family, can begin to free himself or herself from addiction through an empowerment process. Even more importantly, he or she can begin to work toward finding and accepting the self and toward building satisfying human relationships.

The same potential exists for people to free themselves from "organizational addiction," a dependency that can be established around autocratic or paternalistic systems of control (Schael & Fassel, 1988). Programs have been initiated to help people gain a sense of empowerment to counter their "corporate alienation." Like all self-help programs, they teach responsibility and self-respect, important building blocks for an empowered organization. To develop toward empowerment, individuals need a strong sense of their own competence; self-worth; and independence of external control, whether substance or circumstance. The increasing numbers of people who have recovered successfully in such programs can help us find a new vision of our organizations so as to prevent such dependencies. It has become clear that while autocratic or paternalistic systems rely on inducing employees to conform to a corporate culture, such an environment seldom produces an experience of connectedness. Empowering organizations, on the other hand, nurture a positive self-regard that leads to a genuine feeling of connectedness to others.

THE SPIRITUAL CRISIS

The crisis of alienation can be seen as one step toward what some believe is a global crisis that explains all the others, the crisis of spirituality. In recent decades, as the human race has for the first time been forced to face its own mortality, questions about the meaning of life are being asked by more and more people. At first glance these "spiritual" questions might seem to have no place in a discussion of modern organizational life and management. Yet our doubt that spirituality is relevant to such a large part of our lives indicates that there is indeed a spiritual crisis in our midst. If our daily lives and our work relationships convey no spiritual meaning, they provide us with no real sense of purpose or power. The time we spend at work then becomes time when we are not fully human, when we are expected to behave mechanically in our relationships to our work and our coworkers

This crisis, like the preceding crisis of alienation, offers us an opportunity to search for our own essence and to experience empowerment. Research on the "work spirit" phenomenon and the search for spiritual roots in work offers hope that we can integrate our organizational lives with who we are as whole persons (Connelly, 1988; Harvey, 1974; Vaill, 1982). The search for spiritual meaning need not be relegated to a Sunday service; in fact, finding one's work spirit, or the meaning in work, lies at the foundation of the actualized empowerment process. The opportunity now exists for organizations to structure and for managers to encourage empowerment processes that help themselves and their employees find a sense of purpose in their work and integrate it into their entire life experience. The result, a personal relationship with work grounded in a spiritual base, is an essential antecedent of individual empowerment and a necessary prerequisite for the development of high-performance organizations.

Out of this new conception of humanness in the work place will emerge a new definition of leadership that is congruent with the empowerment process. Like each of the other opportunities of crisis we have considered, the crisis of spirituality points clearly to the need for a new conceptual approach and requires us to re-examine and recreate our personal, organizational, and international systems and practices. Before moving on to a detailed description of an empowerment system and its methods, we need to consider the implications of the empowerment construct for the managerial role.

LEADERSHIP FOR EMPOWERMENT

 Overview

Chapter 3 provides a new definition of leadership and power in the light of an emerging organizational and social vision — that of empowerment. It describes six managerial skills — informing, decision making, planning, evaluating, motivating, and developing — and presents six illustrations of how empowering managers use them. The chapter concludes with a discussion of the control issue and provides some general considerations for organizations as they take their first steps toward empowerment.

If we reconceive power as something that is within a person and that can be created as well as distributed, we will need to shift our thinking about management from an emphasis on control to concern for empowerment. When the empowerment process takes hold, the demands for effective leadership are considerably increased. Behind this statement lies a basic dilemma.

For some years writers and social critics have bemoaned the lack of national leaders in the United States (Peters & Waterman, 1982; Bennis & Nanus, 1985). In Sweden the leadership vacuum has even become a social issue and a matter of public discussion. In neither country have the answers that so many seek been forthcoming. One reason is that, in today's world of emerging pluralism, participation, and a higher valuation of human independence and capability, leadership, like power, needs to be reconceptualized. The roots of recent thinking about leadership, while evident in social and political trends, have been most fruitfully explored in the applied behavioral sciences (see Chapter 4).

An empowering leadership concept does not focus exclusively on the "individual manager as hero" but looks at the group or organization development process as a whole (Bradford & Cohen, 1984). On occasion, of course, an individual manager suggests a new direction and takes the lead in moving a system toward it. But rarely does one individual embody such a thrust or exemplify a whole system. The system's daily leadership usually comes, and many say it should come, from throughout the organization.

The classic group dynamics studies of the 1940s demonstrated that a democratic and shared form of leadership is most effective when the tasks and personnel are well matched to each other (Lewin, 1947; Lippitt & White, 1958). In tomorrow's world of faster and more complex change, the need for decentralized leadership is even more obvious. An effective work team is, by definition, one in which the differentiation of members' talents and skills provides the most capable and appropriate leadership for each part of the task at hand. Leadership thus moves from person to person as people's talents and the demands of the situation dictate.

Empowered organizations will move in the same fashion when systems have developed to act quickly (not just to react) as circumstances require. An organization whose leaders are allowed to exercise their empowered status to deal with new situations will build a far stronger leadership infrastructure than a system relying on traditional hierarchical structures or bureaucracies.

However, no such development can occur if control is the central managerial concern. In an empowered organization, the paramount issues become coordination, integration, and facilitation — not control. The manager as facilitator must understand clearly that his or her primary role function is to get the right leadership talents to the right place. This new role, for which few traditional systems of reward or recognition are in place, does not validate the manager's ego through control of others; rather it produces feelings of self-worth by allowing and encouraging and assisting others to get the job done. In an empowered organization the primary role of the manager is not to be *the* problem solver, technical expert, or conductor but the facilitator, the person who fosters the organization's development through active participation, coordination, and permitting others to provide the specific leadership skill(s) needed.

This role calls for a psychologically healthy manager. But it also demands that the stress, confusion, conflict, and alienation crises be used effectively as opportunities to develop the skills of everyone in the organization. As noted in Chapter 2, these crises can help forge the strengths needed for an empowered organization. Because the demands made on employees in democratic or empowered organizations are far broader than those in more traditional systems, considerable time and attention are necessary to prepare employees for their responsibilities (Kieffer, 1984; Kanter, 1983; Murrell, 1977).

In the United States the pluralistic and democratic framework of government created by the Constitution has set the stage on which the empowerment process is being developed. The empowerment process has the potential to prepare our country for the coming waves of change; it can exemplify a new, even a revolutionary, democratic ethic. Such a democratic ethic of power and responsibility is available as a solution to most of our current crises in both economic and sociological areas of concern. It is, in essence, an empowerment philosophy. Although we have too often forgotten how far this ethic has taken our country in its short history, we now have an opportunity to return to the roots of democracy, liberation, and empowerment. To use the power created in a democratic process is to take full advantage of the empowerment potential of ourselves and our organizations.

To do so, managers and other organizational leaders need to be fully aware of how organizations function and what can be done to help them reach their empowered performance potentials. In the following discussion the authors delineate the particular managerial roles necessary to create empowered organizations and provide illustrations of effective managers who are helping empower their associates.

THE MANAGER'S EMPOWERMENT ROLE

If organizations are going to develop the capacity to use their valuable human resources fully and gain a competitive edge, a manager who can facilitate that development is essential. If this opportunity to help our companies compete on a global basis is lost, or if our organizations seek only a technological solution, then the social and international crises we now face will multiply.

The fantasy of a high-tech solution that does not take into account the human or "high touch" component (Naisbitt, 1984) has considerable appeal to those seeking a quick fix or a messiah in the form of a super computer. Yet any adequate high-tech solution can only originate in an organization whose management system values and educates toward that end. As the unfortunate space shuttle *Challenger* disaster so dramatically illustrated, high-tech operations are only as strong as their weakest link; and this weak link has often been the organization's failure to listen to itself. The recent Iranian airline fiasco in the Persian Gulf provides yet another example of the danger of relying on high-tech solutions within rigid hierarchial organizations unable to tolerate high levels of ambiguity and unwilling to permit dispersal of responsibility. In both disasters lower-level decision makers were aware of the errors being made, but their perceived lack of power and responsibility encouraged them to pass all decisions on to high commands; in the few cases when they did attempt to communicate their concerns, they were ignored or overruled. An unrealistic trust in high-tech solutions often encourages managers to take actions that manifest clearly the inability of one person to manage a complex, fast-breaking situation. Ever more redundant levels of technical solutions and quality checkpoints will have minimal effect if the control orientation continues to dominate and the core issues of responsibility, ethics, and power are not reconsidered. To move toward empowerment an organization must rethink its basic assumptions, especially the human dimensions of decision making and the notion of shared responsibility.

The manager's new role, therefore, is to restore a balance between high tech and high touch and to bring before the organization the "softer" issues of morality, ethics, and human competence and worth. He or she will need to establish a new ethic of shared responsibility to help build and develop an infrastructure that facilitates each employee's ability to handle expanded responsibilities. In essence, the role of the manager is to develop the organization's overall skills in each of six management functions. What follows is a discussion of the six — informing, decision making, planning, evaluating, motivating, and developing — that make up this infrastructure (see Figure 2).

FIGURE 2.   The Opportunities of Crises

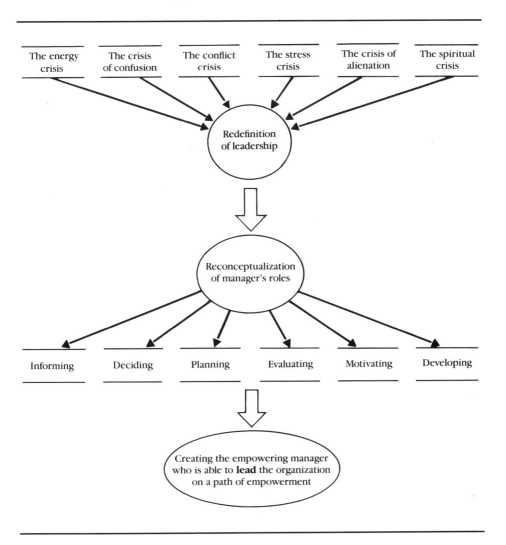

The Empowered Manager's Informational Role

Nothing is so vital to the success of an organization as its ability to gather, analyze, and distribute information. The empowering manager must be able to help establish and maintain not only the technical side of the information equation, but also an open climate of trust that enables information to move smoothly through the organization. Research on the information process suggests that a high level of personal trust is essential to the flow of valid information (Gibb, 1978). A climate or tone of trust that values individual input, operational information, and personal/group assessment and perspective can dramatically enhance an organization's ability to develop into an empowered organization. Low-trust organizations, on the other hand, are notorious for blocking information flow and for political climates that create guarded and distorted information exchange, which can threaten an organization's very existence.

Good information is one of the best examples of a renewable resource: the more there is, the more can be generated. To empower an organization the manager must assume responsibility for informing group members of all data relevant to their jobs, as well as information about the strategic and spiritual essence of the organization. The manager is something like a neuron connector, passing along power so that others can respond as quickly and effectively as possible. He or she must also create feedback mechanisms and interactive systems of communication to reinforce the network linkages made possible by our modern information technologies. However, responsibility for improving the flow belongs not just to the manager but to every person in the organization. Instead of playing the role of quick-fix specialist, the manager should facilitate identification of problems, help solve them, and work to improve the communication climate. The following vignette describes one method an empowered manager used to do all these things.

❖ **Case Vignette 1.**   *Informational Processes That Empower*

> Jason was a master at using information to help empower the work group he managed. Every Monday at approximately 10:30 A.M. the staff of seven technical experts and two support people filled their coffee cups and moved to Jason's office. After checking in with each person to see how he or she was doing and reviewing major activities for the week, Jason proceeded to provide as much data as he felt was useful, or as had been requested, about company concerns or events and anything else that might affect the group's activities. When he had information specifically relevant to the work of only one or a few staff members, he would mention it briefly and request time following the meeting to go into more detail with those directly involved.
>
> Jason prepared for the meeting by chasing down information he thought would be useful; he intentionally erred on the side of providing

too many rather than too few details. As he often asked people what they would like to know, he was frequently reporting on earlier inquiries. Although this was not the only time Jason provided the staff with information, it was a set time, which all respected, to exchange important information. As the weekly gatherings were short, seldom more than thirty minutes, it was often necessary to hold other meetings of the whole group or some part of it to pursue discussions or collect information about particular topics.

Jason's weekly briefings paid off on a number of occasions. Because members were well informed, the group made better decisions about how to accomplish particular tasks. The meetings also provided a forum for the airing of human needs or feelings and for responding to them before they became grievances.

On several occasions these briefings were held without Jason, and they went smoothly; everyone had been trained to share necessary information. When a decision had to be made in his absence, the group handled the task particularly well as they had all the background information needed to make a sound decision. Members of the group felt powerful, for they knew a good deal about the organization's concerns and were sure that Jason would do everything he could to get the right information to the right person at the right time. Jason himself viewed his managerial role as a service rather than a control function, and the success of his empowered staff was recognized throughout the organization.

Information as power, when it is shared, creates more power in a system that encourages and rewards collaboration. Managers need to persuade their coworkers that the whole organization must devote the time and energy necessary to develop and clarify information-sharing guidelines and procedures that will make information an empowerment device.

The Empowered Manager's Decision-Making Role

In traditional hierarchial organizations, the majority of decisions are made near or at the top of the organization by a few people. In turbulent times, however, with so much change and complexity, this is not always the best approach. The Japanese *ringshi* method is a decision process that is slow in formulation but usually gains a time advantage in implementation. In this process a proposed decision is reviewed at all levels of the organization before top-level management puts it into effect. Workers' suggested changes to the proposal are based on their particular expertise and experience.

An empowering manager works in a similar way, building in both a review process and, as the hierarchy is flattened, a decision-making method that reaches downward in the organization. In an empowered organization the location for the final decision can be moved to the point that is most appropriate in terms of information, expertise, and need. An added benefit is that people who have actively participated in making a decision will feel a heightened responsibility for developing a successful outcome.

Although it need not be cumbersome or excessively time consuming, this sort of decision making does have to be carefully designed ahead of time. After the organization has decided on its operational philosophy and encouraged the norms, skills, and rewards needed to institute it, the empowering manager goes to work. Because speed is almost always a critical factor in decision making, the manager prepares the ground in advance, helping develop effective guidelines delineating not only the decision participants but also the method of decision making under a number of different — perhaps unexpected — circumstances.

With an empowering style, more input is sought, and, where possible, the power and responsibility for a decision are shared openly by all those who will be affected by it. Such a process enhances an organization's ability to reach its goals by reducing the "we-they" distinction so often encountered between those who make decisions and those who implement them. As in the Japanese method, a final decision may come about more slowly, but the speed, coordination, and commitment of the implementation phases often make up for it.

To institute a more open decision process, however, a developmental perspective is helpful. A decision needs to be viewed as an entity — from recognition, to planning, to implementing, to evaluating, to generalizing for the "next time." A transition plan with training for increased responsibilities is usually a necessity; asking people to make decisions without the relevant understanding and experience is counterproductive. The following vignette illustrates how a group of new decision makers reached a risk-filled decision that had ramifications for each member's work and personal life.

❖ **Case Vignette 2.** *Decision Making That Empowers*

One of the smaller divisions of a large paper-processing company was scheduled to be closed in the not-too-distant future. The employees of the plant were informed by company headquarters that they could either move 400 miles to a similar operation or leave the company. At first the decision seemed to be a matter of individual choice, but as they met with their local management group they identified another option. They could decide as a group to negotiate purchase of the plant and save their jobs, although it would require them to invest much of their future salaries as start-up capital. The government was willing to help them create an employee stock ownership plan (ESOP), but the major risk, and thus the decision, was all theirs. They discussed and argued over every aspect of the decision until they reached consensus and decided to start their own company.

The empowerment they experienced from taking control of their own destiny produced an organization that, in both climate and performance, exceeded what they had achieved as part of the larger company. This group of sixty people had decided to take full responsibility for themselves, and their economic success was clearly the product of that decision. Their decision to stand together unified them, and their decision to be fully responsible empowered them.

The Empowered Manager's Planning Role

The manager's role in planning is to involve as many as possible of the people whose inputs and interest will help ensure a successful planning process. Participative planning, as the authors have noted, is neither the easiest nor the fastest way for an organization to sort out its plans; but if devotion and commitment to the plans are expected, it is usually necessary. This is particularly true in the early stages of empowerment, when it is desirable to give as many people as possible opportunities to influence the system — so that they realize they can actually do so. As different steps of the process require different knowledge and interests, the empowering manager needs to make the closest match between task and skills, while ensuring that each person is aware of his or her contribution to the plan.

The planning process is almost always discussed in connection with the organization's vision or mission statement — the purpose of its existence. It is imperative, therefore, that members have an opportunity to refine, comment on, or even alter this design for deciding the future. It is equally important that the empowering manager capture the spirit of the members and help create a shared image of what the organization can become. The vision created by planning can inspire and empower members, creating a shared commitment to accomplish the planning goals.

Moreover, the planning process can be more than a once-a-year event carried out by a distant staff group. An empowering planning process depends on the manager to involve others in conceiving and achieving the vision; by translating it into the group's daily work he or she links everyone's everyday tasks with a broader meaning. All members need to know that they are part of an overall plan and need to be able to identify their own unique contributions to its accomplishment. The following vignette describes how one sales manager used the planning process to inspire and empower her sales staff.

❖ **Case Vignette 3.** *Planning Approaches That Empower*

Annual sales forecasts for Sarah's group had always been created by the headquarters staff located five hundred miles away. Each year she was told that a 7-percent increase, give or take a few percentage points, would be their goal. When a new vice president joined the company, however, he instituted a number of decentralized decisions, including the next year's planning process. Headquarters notified Sarah that she would have to generate her own sales projections and operational plan, including a recommended budget to support it.

Sharing this information with the sales people, Sarah informed them that they would create the annual sales forecasts together. For the first time, the planning process became real to them. In the course of working together, the staff members shared ideas about strategies and programs as they had never done before; they divulged not only their last year's sales but also their target figures for the next year. The open exchange of information made it more acceptable to ask for and offer help to each other. The ambitious plan they worked out projected a sales increase of 13 percent. They actually accomplished an increase of a little less than 10 1/2 percent, which compared favorably with the preceding year's increase of 7 1/4 percent.

Much of the difference was attributed to a phenomenon fairly well supported in the research literature: people who set their own goals tend to expect more of themselves. The group's improved performance was also linked to the empowered feeling resulting from an open and participatory planning process.

The Empowered Manager's Evaluator Role

One of the most difficult roles managers have to perform is that of evaluator. Unfortunately, what was conceived as a method to help employees realize their potential has often been turned into a process of finding fault. An empowering evaluative system, however, builds on the process of "valuing" and takes advantage of what is learned in the process to improve performance. Empowerment provides managers with two ways to avoid the trap of the "critic's role."

The first, described in the recent organization development literature (Cooperrider, 1986) and in earlier discussions of third-world development (Murrell, 1984b), emphasizes the system's strengths. Avoiding a problem-centered focus, it uses positive and healthy energies as primary guides for an organization's growth, development, and planning. The same strategy applied to the individual would focus on particular talents to help him or her identify opportunities for using them more effectively.

The second evaluation strategy is a self-diagnostic technique in which a manager gives support and encouragement in response to an employee's request. When a person identifies an area of growth or a potential opportunity, the empowering manager's job is to assist, not to record a deficiency as a threat to future prospects. The control process can then become internal to the system and to the individual, who can request help when a goal is not being achieved rather than attempting to cover up a limitation. Managers in this role have to learn how to help people ask for help by creating many opportunities for them to reflect on their work. Most people, however, are not accustomed to self-assessment; they expect others to tell them about their strengths and deficiencies and set goals for them. Empowering managers thus need to help people recognize the value of self-assessment as well as to model the technique. Although an empowering manager does not withhold his or her perspective from the employee, it is the individual who decides what to do with that piece of information.

Management best performs its evaluative role by establishing control systems that respond to calls for assistance and do not raise the specter of future punishments. The following vignette examines how well two organizations' evaluation systems met these criteria and contrasts their results.

 Case Vignette 4. *Evaluating as Empowering*

> Once a year ten middle-level managers of Company X are given a standard performance evaluation and are required to administer it to their own staffs. Policy demands that members be rank ordered according to their performance on six scales. As this occurs in early January, what little team spirit or company morale remains from the Christmas holidays is quickly dissipated. Although the results are officially secret — like much information in the company — the competitive rankings are the topic of rumor and gossip for many weeks. Company X's evaluation system creates considerable internal competition; many people feel like losers in a process that does not value their contributions.
>
> In Company Y a performance evaluation process occurs quarterly. Discussions between manager and employee involve self-evaluation, a manager-initiated process of valuing and showing appreciation, and a written contract identifying what is necessary to improve or sustain performance in the next three months. Company Y is able to empower its people to improve performance, and its reward systems are set up to encourage team work and cooperation.

The Empowered Manager's Motivating Role

Pride in accomplishment is a very powerful motivator; in a work environment, it is the essence of empowerment. Since research indicates that the strongest motivation factors, like pride, are intrinsic, the empowering manager does not rely on extrinsic incentives like pay or punishment but sets an example worthy of emulation. Empowering by example, however, is more than being a role model; it is also being available to coach, counsel, and direct and to help structure the organization so that its reward systems are consistent with its goals. The goal of a motivating style of empowerment is not to create automatons but to develop self-motivated individuals. Recognizing that the organization knows and appreciates their individuality and special talents allows people to perform their assignments with confidence.

Motivation, like evaluation, is at the core of the empowerment process. Although humans are intrinsically motivated, much of their self-insight is buried under many layers of external pressure and experiences that have blocked them from discovering their personal life values. In the transition to an empowered system, therefore, managers need to learn how to help people become more aware of their own goals so that they can actively participate in and eventually guide their own motivation. Managers, in this role, must know about motivation — its theory, types, and process — in order to facilitate self-insight on behalf of their organization's achievement.

❖ **Case Vignette 5.** *Motivating Empowerment*

> Each person on a professional team at Data Systems General (DSG) is specially selected for his or her ability to identify and successfully accomplish self-defined goals. DSG's commitment to team building and developing interpersonal skills in all its people allows it to function as a highly productive organization and not a collection of individual stars. The founders of DSG, two very bright computer scientists, both led platoons of highly trained and motivated Israeli soldiers. Although one of the founders grew up in a kibbutz and the other was from the city, their similar war service convinced them of the importance of team work. As young lieutenants they were assisted in forming their fighting units by a staff specialist trained in psychology and leadership.
>
> After leaving the service the two young men combined their computer expertise and their military experience to design a company that included both computer experts and specialists in motivation who could help in choosing and developing the work teams. These teams were extremely successful and soon were providing computer services to an international market. The training of these highly motivated employees, who came from all over the world, gave equal emphasis to updating their technical skills and developing interpersonal skills. Their high motivation levels were maintained by teamwork that was empowering in its results for the organization and beneficial for the employees. As an empowered organization DSG set a model as a mini-multinational firm likely to be successful in the global economy of the 1990s.

To reconceptualize leadership as everyone's responsibility is to set the stage for organizational maturity and achievement of full potential. The sense of shared responsibility created will help empower the organization and fill the leadership vacuum, not by becoming dependent on a few great leaders but by creating more power and more leadership potential in a larger number of people.

The Empowered Manager's Development Role

A fully empowered organization is one that uses all the skills and ideas that people can contribute while assuring its continual growth and survival by responding to a changing external environment. It is essential, therefore, that the empowering manager's unique set of daily tasks be developmental in perspective. He or she always must be searching for ways to make improvements, constantly working with people to develop even higher levels of performance in the future. This progressive perspective is not simply one of quantity or quality, although both are important; developmental improvements emerge out of a higher level of organizational functioning that results from better coordination and integration. This higher level of functioning also derives from the manager's skills in informing, decision making, planning, evaluating, and motivating. The test of an empowering manager is not his or her own functioning but the capacity of the system and the organization to respond and grow in an ever-more-challenging world. The manager as facilitator is judged by how much better *others* can perform the traditional management activities. In the future, management's main contribution will be to create systems that are participatory and self-managing. The professionals in such organizations will be able to meet both their own spiritual and motivational needs and the increasing demands of the outside world.

This developmental perspective is also key to the long-range strategy that increases an organization's growth and survival capacity. Traditional managers are principally concerned with moving from a short-term strategy of profit maximization to a mid-term strategy of producing needed products at higher and higher levels of quality. Empowered managers, however, also think in terms of creating a better, more effectively developing organization. They glean their sense of well-being from helping themselves, others, and the organization attain both present and future effectiveness. Self-serving managers, who block others' contributions and the system's growth, cannot accomplish these broader goals. Self-serving power, in McClelland's term "the negative face of power," will not help establish the more effective and powerful organizations we need to assure our future prosperity (McClelland, 1970).

Innovative and creative new start-up firms, and some older organizations willing to risk the investment in empowering their people, are showing the way of success. A manager in a profession that demands leadership needs to read the writing on the wall and to start establishing the specific skills of empowerment, including an orientation toward development.

❖ **Case Vignette 6.**   *Developing as the Empowering Role*

> Every employee of this company has a development plan that emphasizes career goals but also sets out the training, experience, and growth in skills needed to progress in the organization. These plans are examined twice a year and revised and updated as necessary. Some employees' pace of change is slower than others, some have career plans that include temporary leaves, and some are encouraged to take sabbaticals.
>
> The company is known as an empowering organization, and its flexibility and creativity make it a model company for firms operating in a postindustrial and increasingly global information and service economy. The atmosphere of vitality produced by well-informed employees charting their own course of development with the organization's support and encouragement is energizing. Thousands of candidates apply for any job that opens up — proof, on one level, that the development process is paying off. The other obvious payoff is in the power that has been created in the organization by people working hard to achieve not only the organization's strategic plans but also their own goals, which almost always coincide with the organizational direction set by the participatory planning process.

 ──

CONCLUDING POINTS: THE EMPOWERMENT PARADOX AND PATH

Organizations built on control and not on an empowering perspective seem to be finding it very difficult to respond to the new challenges of global competition. Often they pay very high salaries but do not reap a commensurate return. They are frequently organizations bloated with layer upon layer of redundant employees competing with organizations with half as many levels of management. They are organizations that hire the best and brightest young professionals, only to see them leave in short order because of their stifling rules and control orientation. They are the organizations being outmaneuvered by young mavericks, savvy foreign competitors with lower labor costs, and their own employees who break away and establish competing firms. Such control-oriented and bureaucratic organizations ("corpocracies" as others have called them) are not developing either internally or in terms of new markets, and their days are numbered.

Clearly global economic challenges require organizations that are more effective and far more powerful. The paradox is that to create such organizations managers must first give up control. To give up a strongly entrenched belief in something so fundamentally a part of management thinking as control requires tremendous faith. It is unlikely that any traditional manager would spontaneously turn into an empowering manager; in any case, colleagues and employees would probably greet a rapid change in management style with high levels of distrust, disbelief, and cynicism. The empowering path is a long one, and the first step must be a mental one, which will slowly lead toward confidence in the rightness and effectiveness of the process.

In that initial step a manager should look carefully at how far along the path to empowerment the organization has already traveled. How much freedom and responsibility do the "best" people exercise? Are they not already the high performers and do they not already have power as a result? Do they not also empower their manager because of their performance and productivity? This is the essence of the empowerment paradox: by giving the most effective people freedom to develop, the organization gains a great deal. To gain more power for the organization, however, trust and faith must be extended to *all* employees; for all those not trusted consume inordinate amounts of time and energy in terms of managerial efforts to control them. The organization hardly breaks even on them because whatever they produce has been cajoled from them, at great cost, in a zero-sum exchange: their contribution minus the manager's efforts.

The paradox of empowerment is a self-fulfilling prophecy much like McGregor's idea that managers regard people as either X, needing control, or Y, motivated (McGregor, 1960). If I view others as needing control and impose limits on their power, I create a dependency state for them that will *require* a Theory X management style. They can only break out of this adolescent position by open rebellion, making it almost impossible to reach an agreement based on shared responsibility.

If, as the authors have argued, power is not a finite resource but one that can be created, it follows that for an organization to gain in power, every member must become more powerful. In reality, of course, one rarely finds a manager genuinely interested in sharing power. Yet to do so in exchange for a total increase in the effectiveness of the organization is to move to a higher understanding about power. In any case, the ability to command obedience is already a rapidly disappearing commodity. What member of a highly educated and skilled work force will tolerate being commanded? And what kind of organization finds it necessary to use power this way with people who care about their work?

After surveying the degree of empowerment already in place, a manager moving toward an empowering style can consider how to change his or her approach to employees whose performance is less than superior. A review of the six managerial roles discussed earlier can provide a good starting point for this examination. For example, what problems in evaluation and development might prevent people from meeting their obligation to make the organization function more effectively? How does the manager's way of structuring his or her roles affect the relationship with these employees? What changes can each side reasonably expect the other to make? These are the sorts of questions to ask, and answer, to start down the empowerment path.

Finally, what about the rest of the organization? If it seems likely that an empowerment approach will succeed within one group, how can a manager use it to understand the rest of the organization? Of course, in a deeply entrenched political climate of distrust, it will be a long, hard, and perhaps impossible road to empowerment. Organizational culture changes slowly; but within a particular area of responsibility it can do so, assuming that a manager is proficient in protecting himself or herself and the group from the zero-sum political games of self-serving strategists outside the unit. In interacting with coworkers in other areas it is essential to explain clearly the empowerment strategy being implemented and to give specific examples of how empowering actions can improve the organization's overall effectiveness. Unless an organization is mired in its own self-serving ethic, the logic of the empowerment paradox should at least arouse interest. If not, exit may be the only reasonable choice. Many people, however, misread the attitudes of their organizations and other managers; frequently such people are unwilling to initiate new ideas themselves but will respond to new leadership when its effectiveness is demonstrated.

Truly empowered managers are not naive; they are politically astute. They are also risk takers smart enough to know when the organization will not support their efforts and, therefore, when they must make the choice to stay or to leave. Even this choice is not simple to empowered managers but is carefully considered in terms of their own needs, the needs of coworkers, and those of the organization to which they have committed themselves. An empowered manager is an empowered *person* with a whole-self, ethical framework that makes all of his or her interactions important.

The requirements for an organization about to take the empowerment path are more involved than the decisions a single manager might make. The organization must first look seriously at how it functions in the six areas just described and then choose, very consciously and explicitly, how it prefers to operate within each area. Managers can assist this self-examination if they and the organization are willing to look openly at themselves. The risks of requesting feedback, of really looking at oneself and the organization, are not small; the more resistant to giving power to its people the organization has been in the past, the more difficult the transition will be.

The manager's job in helping achieve a successful transition from control to empowerment will take not only considerable courage but also knowledge that the organization's long-term survival depends on building awareness of its own developmental processes and ability to create power. Growth will not be easy; a radical shift in the power paradigm will bring once-hidden conflicts to the surface and force tough decisions about sharing responsibility. Power and responsibility are by necessity tied together; it will be the manager's role to facilitate the making of new contracts about the nature of this relationship.

In many organizations there is no internal ideal to inspire and motivate employees and to lend a direction for development. The empowerment goal is meant to help provide such an ideal. In the next chapter the authors take this general discussion of empowerment a step further by looking at the psychological, educational, organizational, and managerial foundations of empowerment.

FOUNDATIONS OF THE CONCEPT OF EMPOWERMENT

 Overview

Chapter 4 begins with a discussion of the world's readiness to accept an empowerment perspective. It explores early contributions to the empowerment concept in the psychological, educational, motivational, and organizational literature and in the experience of participants in the civil rights movement, volunteerism, higher education, third world societies, the women's movement, and health care systems. It then surveys recent research in motivation and in six areas central to current thinking on empowerment: values, leadership, environment, adult learning theory, structure, and integration.

THE SOCIAL CONTEXT OF EMPOWERMENT

A solid foundation for empowerment in theory and experience has been generated in the social sciences and in various social movements during the past five decades. Without those building blocks empowerment would probably not have emerged so readily in response to the crises surveyed in Chapter 2. A survey of these antecedents of empowerment can serve as an excellent starting point for managers and organizations thinking about building an empowered self or system.

To conceptualize empowerment as a personal or organizational phi-

41

losophy it is helpful to look at how it has evolved in particular social arenas. The civil rights movement, especially black voter registration drives and political activism, have stimulated several studies of how a group can overcome powerlessness and discrimination and gain democratic rights (Solomon, 1976; Perry, 1980). Similarly, sociologists have seen empowerment at work in the community and neighborhood development (Fainstein & Martin, 1978; Perlman, 1979) and United Farm Worker (Hoffman, 1978) movements. Berger and Neuhaus (1977) have studied the ways mediating structures of family, church, neighborhoods, and voluntary associations might empower citizens and decrease powerlessness through nongovernmental forms of empowerment. Their model does not focus on specific issues or rights, but looks for ways in which people can change and improve their worlds by using their own resources and capacities to learn. Like the youth self-advocacy project described in Chapter 2, the key is to see people not as pawns or passive recipients but as makers of social policy and reform, as agents of change.

A parallel movement in the voluntary social services emphasizes a shift from service, through advocacy, to empowerment (O'Connell, 1978) that is consistent with a broader cultural trend toward decentralization (Naisbitt, 1982). Although this trend coincides with basic democratic beliefs, it depends for its success on the opportunity for hopeless and desperate people to gain authentic power. Individuals need to care enough to help create this new power; but if society as a whole feels threatened by it, it will probably not be attained. When power is seen as a zero-sum eventuality, society turns against itself; if empowerment occurs, it builds itself.

Kieffer (1984) points to the need for "participatory competence" for all citizens in a democracy and has prepared a rough model of how empowerment occurs in stages or "eras." He asks exciting new questions such as "What are, and how do we develop, the participatory competencies needed to live in a complex democratic society?" Murrell (1977), after three years of firsthand observation of two uniquely innovative organizations, came to the same conclusion as Kieffer: in a democracy all members of an organization or community, not just managers or leaders, need to possess participative skills.

Most experts agree that our present educational system does not focus on preparing our youth to live in such an active democracy; it may be that these participative skills presuppose a notion of empowerment and a philosophy of democracy as essential for social action. There is, however, growing agreement in the educational literature that some version of an empowerment philosophy is crucial to effective teaching (Robertson, 1978); no other profession has as its specific goal the creation of responsible adults and citizens with the capacity to accomplish social ends. In the professional management literature too, several writers have given increased attention to empowerment as an antidote to bureaucratic malaise. Peter Block's collection of practitioner recommendations (1987) provides in-depth, practical lessons for managers who want to choose an empowerment path. It brings to the expanding field of management literature new insights grounded in years of successful organization development (OD) consulting.

In the growing literature of third-world development, frequent discussions of empowerment are occurring. Brinkerhoff (1979) and Bryant (1982) both devote attention to the need for developing countries to empower their citizens in order to improve not only the economic but also the sociocultural conditions of their societies. An OD approach to third world development would use the natural strengths of a society to empower local organizations and their managers (Murrell, 1984). The empowerment theme runs strongly through all this literature as a way of breaking free of the colonial legacy of rigid bureaucratization and developing home-grown solutions to critical problems. Mahatma Gandhi's ability to lead a whole nation toward empowerment is a similar model of social change that departs radically from both violent revolution and top-down control.

Within the women's movement too, empowerment has been given considerable attention. Women academics and consultants (Cunningham, 1985; Kanter, 1977; Moglen, 1983) have analyzed their personal experiences with power in large organizations. They point out that managers who empower their subordinates not only can assist both men and women but also can help reverse the recent productivity problems in American industry. As organizations become less male dominated, both sexes will need advice and counsel on developing personal power (Barnett, 1981). The entry of more women into the work force, like the earlier progress of minority groups, is just a beginning. Once entry is gained, women's opportunities for successful and satisfying careers will depend on their ability to avoid the alienation so often associated with work in large organizations (Walker, 1988).

Finally, in the health care field, professionals are advocating the patients' informed responsibility, an emphasis that seems likely to continue (Stensrud & Stensrud, 1982). Further changes will probably occur as patients become empowered and preventive health aids and self-diagnostic practices become better known and more widely available. The present focus on remedial services is moving toward the prevention of illness and, through educational and informational methodologies, the promotion of wellness.

In all these fields, the basic concern derives from the individual's drive for self-empowerment and tries to define what people must do or experience to develop their power (Loughary & Ripley, 1982). This liberating concept has deep roots in Western philosophy and in current psychological and sociological thinking. John McCluskey (1976), in his review of the power literature, with its emphasis on control, coercion, and dominance, finds historical support for the concept of liberating power in the writings of Plato, Sir Thomas More, Jean-Jacques Rousseau, and Karl Marx; he also identifies partial support for the idea in the work of such modern-day social scientists as Dorwin Cartwright, Alvin Zander, Amitai Etzioni, and others. Various forms of empowerment are being explored by organizational sociologists like Loughary and McCluskey and by leaders in the field of organization development like Edgar Schein, Jay Galbraith, and Rosabeth Moss Kanter. All these writers support an empowering concept with regard to social change and personal benefits as well as economic development.

When the American Indians faced environmental challenges or pressures from other groups, they turned to their Guardian Spirit for empowerment. When modern men and women face increasing demands, they turn not to a spirit, but to that uniquely human talent, problem solving. This skill allows the human animal to find new solutions to problems through creating power, rather than just distributing it. If, as these writers have argued, power can be reconceptualized as something to be shared *and* created, the empowerment concept may provide the basic skills needed to construct the organizational forms and social institutions necessary for survival in a postindustrial world. Such a radical shift in thinking about power can advance wholly different social systems capable of advancing human evolution another step. If such systems allow human energies to converge synergistically rather than being forced to consume one another in an antiquated zero-sum game, societies can become true havens of human potential, maturity, and well-being.

ROOTS OF EMPOWERMENT

It seems serendipitous that empowerment has come to the fore of American organizational life at this time. The philosophical swing of the 1950s, the self-expression emphasis of the 1960s, the technical focus of the 1970s, and the group and quality models of the 1980s have led steadily toward empowerment. Contributions have come from many writers and fields of study: philosophy (pragmatism, existentialism, phenomenology); psychology (the human potential movement formulated by Abraham Maslow and William Schutz); counseling theory (Carl Rogers); social psychology (group dynamics, interpersonal relationships, Kurt Lewin); management theory (Elton Mayo, Chester Barnard, Chris Argyris, Douglas McGregor); organization theory (Jay Galbraith, Henry Mintzberg); and organization development (personal and organizational congruency, systems view, change theory; Edgar Schein, Richard Beckhard, Jack Gibb, Leland Bradford, and Kurt Lewin).

Publication of Douglas McGregor's *The Human Side of Enterprise* (1960) signaled an historically new integration of this innovative theory into management and organizational thought. In it, the theories of personality and motivation that both led up to and followed its publication began to merge into a view of individual human beings and their value as primary organizational resources. That development led to a renewal of vitality and interest in American work life.

Motivation

Theories of motivation and their applications provided a firm beginning for empowerment. A number of key understandings about human motivation that have evolved in the past forty-plus years have contributed directly to the empowerment concept:

Motivation is an individual matter. Extensive research has demonstrated the complexity and variability of human motivation. The finding that motivation is inherently individual suggests that organizations need to rethink strategies for motivating people according to their unique personal and developmental circumstances; it also heightens the importance of the manager's relations with each individual employee.

The human condition is to strive. Nearly all theories of motivational need recognize that people seek growth and development. Some call this process self-actualization; others call it reaching for a state of equilibrium. Today, the effort to foster a growth orientation has found its niche in human resources departments, in corporate board rooms, in presidential offices, in classrooms, and around family dinner tables. Increasingly, the role of managers, teachers, parents, social workers, and counselors is to help clients, students, children, and employees enhance their self-images and their sense of self-fulfillment. Again, this understanding has made it imperative for managers and organizations to provide an orientation toward growth in the work environment.

The responsibility for human motivation is multidimensional. As motivational theories proliferated, it became clear that the responsibility for motivation does not rest solely with the individual. We have recognized that people do care about what kind of job they do, can grow, and are willing to give that extra effort *when their circumstances allow them to do so.* In any work place there are (at least) three sources of a sense of responsibility: (1) the individual, whose responsibility it is to know his or her self, to grow, to communicate, and to participate; (2) the manager, whose responsibility it is to recognize the employee's individual style, to ask, to listen, to appraise, and to foster growth; (3) the organization, whose responsibility it is to design and implement policies that motivate, to demonstrate commitment to employees, and to support and plan for employee well-being and growth.

Other factors found to affect American organizational life are the importance of self-concept, issues of equity, the environment, managerial assumptions about human nature, the work itself, and motivation as a system of exchange. In short, there is a direct relationship between an individual's sense of well-being and life experiences. Since work, in whatever setting, is central to human existence, our occupational lives directly influence our self-concepts, our motivation; and, in turn, our creativity and productivity. The recognition of this chain of relationships and the effect of particular policies and strategies on it have provided the principal framework for the empowerment construct.

In addition to this connection among self-worth, self-actualization, and organizational life, the concept of empowerment is based on an understanding of human behavior rooted in numerous research studies and the work of several theorists and analysts. Each of the following contributions not only helped define the construct of empowerment but also can be used as a firm foundation for implementing it:

1. *Values:* Chris Argyris' (1955) classic discussion of the management dilemma — company needs versus individual development;

2. *Leadership:* The discussions of Tannenbaum, Kallajian, and Weschler (1954), Bennis (1982), and Lippitt and This (1967) on the characteristics of effective group leaders;

3. *Environment:* Carl Rogers' (1961) work on the environmental climate that allows the facilitative (empowering) processes to become operational;

4. *Adult Learning:* Malcolm Knowles' (1975) description of learning as a life-long process; its implications for the adult learner; and Kolb, Rubin, and McIntyre's (1971) conceptualization of experiential learning;

5. *Organizational Structure:* Jack Gibb's (1964) recognition of the relations among individual needs (e.g., trust), communication, goals, and organizational structure;

6. *Systems Integration:* Recognition of the connections between organizational health and individual welfare and the postwar application of systems analysis to the integration of technological and human systems.

Values

In the 1950s Chris Argyris, a professor of management at Yale University, also acted as a consultant on long-range planning and group decision making to several large corporations. Before long he realized that before an organization can address these issues it must decide to what extent it can develop people and, at the same time, get the job done (Argyris, 1955). The underlying assumption is, of course, that *both* goals are appropriate management aims and that the value dilemma of reconciling them must be resolved by a company's top management before it can consider empowering strategies. Giving high priority to both the worth of individuals and their value in terms of contributions to the organization requires a close examination of the organization's values.

Large organizations, however, have traditionally operated in ways that are counterproductive to individual well-being; those that utilize unity of command, tight control, and task specialization place potentially unhealthy limits on their people. Moreover, recent research has indicated that these operational structures also limit organizational well-being. Empowerment, on the other hand, requires a value-based dialog that culminates in very clear statements about how an organization (1) feels about its employees, (2) sees its mission, (3) is willing to operate, and (4) defines its vision. Taking the time for such a values clarification as a first step will afford a system a firmer foundation for the future. Scott Paper Company has directly addressed this issue of values clarification in its internal document entitled "Exploring the Scott Vision."[1] This blueprint for the future (excerpted here) describes how Scott defines the relationship between company and individual needs and development.

Scott describes how it feels about its employees:

Human resources excellence means we want to effectively develop and utilize the talents of our employees. We believe people are our most valued asset and our greatest competitive advantage.

Buildings and equipment depreciate, while people have the opportunity to grow. We want each employee to grow to his or her full level of ability. We seek to have mutually beneficial, enduring relationships with our employees, and have them feel ownership in their jobs, their units and the entire Company. We want to empower employees to make decisions, to give their best, and to feel proud of what they do.

Scott also defines how it sees its mission:

Part of our Vision is an understanding of our reason for being as a Company. That reason, as we see it, is to continually improve the health and value of Scott in order to create wealth for our stakeholders over time.

First, let's examine that sentence.

Health. If we are to meet our goals, Scott must be healthy in terms of its financial position, talented and dedicated employees, strong market share, superior products and technology, effective cost management and more.

Value. This means Scott must be positioned to deliver good things, in a variety of ways, to all its stakeholders.

Wealth. It means more than just money. It means jobs and rewarding careers. Excellent products, fairly priced, that meet people's needs better than the competition. It calls for Scott's contributing to the communities in which we operate and being a Company that offers rewarding returns for its shareholders.

Our stakeholders. We have many millions of them. They include not only people who own stock and who buy from Scott. People who sell things to Scott, and people in the communities in which we operate our mills and

[1]From "Exploring the Scott Vision" by Scott Paper Company, 1987. Excerpts reprinted by permission of Scott Paper Company.

offices and harvest our timber. And the banks and other institutions that lend us money to grow our business. All of these groups have a stake in Scott.

So, Scott's reason for being is a big part of our Vision.

The other part is our idea of the kind of Company we want to be. We want to be known by our employees and by all others who deal with us as a Company that is healthy ... growing ... prosperous ... willing to not only accept change but to initiate change ... skilled in the management of our assets ... responsible to our stakeholders ... and, simply, a Company acknowledged as the best at what we do.

In addition, Scott discusses how it is willing to operate:

How will we make that Vision a reality?

We will do it by concentrating on three areas: growth, human resources excellence, and stakeholder alignment.

By growth we mean that we will strengthen our basic business by understanding the needs of our customers and end-users better than anyone else and adapting to those needs. We will add new businesses that promise profit and growth. We will shed any parts of our business that are holding us back, or that don't fit with our Vision. Our growth strategy focuses on personal care and cleaning worldwide and on coated printing papers in the U.S.

Finally, our Vision demands that everyone — Scott Paper and all of our stakeholders — be in a win/win situation. Many people suspect that if someone wins in business, someone else has to lose. We don't believe that. If employees are happy in their jobs and proud of their work, and if Scott customers see our products as well worth the money — both these groups have won, and so has Scott.

Scott has a plan for the future. We call it Scott Vision.

We invite you to share it.

In short, this document clearly defines Scott's vision. But it goes beyond definition; it also describes a process that took place in mid-March 1987. "All Scott employees must understand and share in the Vision. To start the process, six Scott employees from around the world met in Philadelphia where they discussed the Vision with Phil Lippincott," Scott's chairperson. They first spent three days with the senior executives of the company who had participated in defining the vision; they learned what the vision meant and the "thinking that went with it." Then they spent a whole day with Lippincott asking questions and clarifying their learnings.

The document concludes with the following statement:

> This is the end of the beginning of exploring the Scott Vision. You will see and hear more about it in the months and years to come. That's because the Vision will not become a reality until you come to know about it, understand it, and share in it.

In this statement, in the title of the document ("Exploring the Scott Vision"), and in the dialog with Lippincott, Scott Paper Company has demonstrated not only the vision itself but also a willingness to continue the process of sharing, examing, and enhancing that vision.

Scott Paper Company has made recognizable strides in the "value" root of empowerment with both its vision statement and its empowering process for sharing the vision. In addition, it has recognized the next root of empowerment, that of leadership. Central to the document's intention is the desire to bring an open, concerned leader to the fore — showing Phil Lippincott as a vision setter and as a participant, both of which are roles that represent the value and leadership roots of empowerment.

Leadership

The conceptualization and implementation of empowerment points clearly to the need for a new style of effective leadership. Important underpinnings for today's definition of empowering leadership has come from the 1960s literature on T-groups. Tannenbaum et al. (1954) has described five behavioral tasks for the group leader, which have direct application for today's empowering manager:

1. *Create situations conducive to learning.* By defining work as a learning situation, we underscore the developmental aspect of empowerment. The leader's role in establishing the necessary learning climate is an essential aspect of empowerment.

2. *Establish a model of behavior.* Leaders' willingness to take risks, change work patterns, recognize their own strengths and limitations, and actively integrate self and work provide others with models from which to "try out" being empowered.

3. *Introduce new values.* Empowered leaders implicitly or explicitly introduce the new values that undergird empowerment. Accepting the validity of value clarification and allowing time for that process are part of the empowering process.

4. *Facilitate the flow of communication.* Empowerment requires in-

formation sharing, especially as it relates to expectations (those of the organization and those of the person). It also requires information relevant to task achievement ("getting the job done in the best possible manner"). As current research has demonstrated, a primary role of the leader is to facilitate information flow. Not fulfilling this role cripples attempts to empower an organization or unit.

5. *Participate as an expert.* The leader's key function is to empower others, often by sharing his or her expertise developed from experience, research, or course work. Knowing *when* to be expert is a critical factor in the empowering process. Too much expertness increases dependency and reduces empowered behaviors; however, sharing expertise to eliminate unhealthy blockages can empower people to move forward.

In 1967, Gordon Lippitt and Les This published an important article listing the variables affecting the trainer's roles in laboratory education settings. Attention to the following factors can also assist leaders who are striving to empower people:

1. Purpose and design of the work (within the total system);
2. Strategies for implementing two-level work designs: empowered self plus healthy work group;
3. Group composition;
4. Practicing (operational) philosophy of the leader;
5. Expectations of group members (employees);
6. The organization's expectations (system, top management, culture);
7. Organizational and personal needs;
8. Influence of the leader's peers and role expectations in general;
9. Current state of research and experience (with empowerment in organizations);
10. Needs of the leader.

T-groups and laboratory education have as their primary goals the facilitation of personal awareness, sensitivity to group dynamics, and personal growth. The underlying assumption is that people who have such experiences will be personally centered and therefore more able to contribute to society in constructive ways. The methods utilized by such learning settings include assuring each person's willingness to participate, self-initiated learning, personal giving and receiving of feedback, examining one's own assumptions about power and authority, and interpersonal skill development. The ethical base is firm: although within the group norms strongly support participation, one is *allowed* to participate, not forced to do so. People *choose* to participate or to leave (physically or emotionally). Empowering leadership operates in a similar interpersonal space that *allows* for the participatory process.

In 1964 Warren Bennis examined the role of change agents — the terms *trainer, facilitator, change agent,* and *consultant* were often used interchangeably in the 1960s — and noted that their actions are normative in nature. That is, the norms initiated are based on the goal of personal enhancement through group-allowed learning. The normative goals with the most relevance in organizational settings are similar (Bennis, 1964, pp. 308–309):

1. Improving the interpersonal competence of managers;
2. Effecting a change in values so that human factors and feelings come to be considered legitimate;
3. Developing increased understanding between and within working groups in order to reduce tensions;
4. Developing more effective team management;
5. Developing better, more rational and open methods of conflict resolution to replace the usual bureaucratic methods of suppression, denial, and the use of naked and unprincipled power;
6. Encouraging organic (versus mechanistic) relationships among and within groups that rely on mutual trust, interdependence, shared responsibility, and conflict resolution through problem solving.

Environment

The question of how an environment acts to empower a group and of how best to create such an environment has recently generated a good deal of research. Like ideas about leadership roles, approaches to the appropriate climate or atmosphere for personal development often evolved in T-groups and laboratory learning settings. Many leaders spent long hours deciding which ways to intervene were most appropriate to the group's membership, the organization's stage of development or stated goals, or the trainer's personal style. They tried to determine what environmental characteristics would provide the optimal conditions for the growth and development of individuals, groups, and organizations.

It was found that the most effective environment is one that is supportive and nonthreatening and backed up by organizational policies that have been clearly communicated to everyone. Organizations must recognize that creating such an environment is time consuming and that operationalizing such a system can range from difficult to impossible, depending on the starting point. Furthermore, it requires a very personal commitment by managers, supervisors, and project directors, who must be able to listen, to give feedback, to express feelings, and to become personally empowered. They must be able to model the difficulties encountered in a transition from an unempowered to an empowered setting and to project the sense of personal well-being and willingness to help others that can be generated in such a situation.

No one spoke more eloquently about the climate-setting function and characteristics of the facilitative relationship than Carl Rogers, both in his client-centered counseling model and his encounter group methodologies. The facilitative relationship as envisioned by Rogers dovetails remarkably well with the requirements for empowerment. Some of these characteristics are:

1. Recognition of the need to establish a facilitative environment;
2. Acceptance of the system in terms of its current status;
3. Acceptance of each individual and the degree of self-knowledge he or she presently possesses;
4. Empathetic understanding, taking the time to concentrate on each person's unique circumstances;
5. Willingness to operate in terms of one's own feelings in the here-and-now and to allow issues to be raised for group consideration;
6. Readiness to give and receive feedback, thus conveying the relevance of each person's input and the importance of open communications for growth;
7. Expressiveness about one's own concerns and problems, thus making the leader a part of the team;
8. Avoidance of planning (letting the issues emerge organically);
9. Avoidance of interpretive comments that attribute motives to behaviors;
10. Recognition of the growth potential of these behaviors within a group setting;
11. Physical movement and contact that is spontaneous, genuine, and appropriate.

Although Rogers defined these behavioral characteristics for counselors and leaders of growth groups, it is apparent that they would go far in creating an environment conducive to empowering others in whatever setting they are adopted.

Learning Theory

The concept of life-long learning is central to empowerment and emerged at about the same time as the human potential perspectives and motivation constructs considered in Chapter 3. Believing that healthy human beings are constantly striving for self-development and are able and willing to continue learning, Malcolm Knowles (1975) initiated the discussion about adult learning theory. Some major tenets of his learning theory are that adults:

1. Learn when what they are learning is relevant to them.
2. Learn best when the climate or atmosphere for learning is nonjudgmental and supportive.
3. Learn when they are committed (i.e., to the learning, to their own growth, to the organization, to others).
4. Learn when they understand the personal context of new learning (Where am I now? Where am I going? How will I get there?). They want a map of the world as well as a roadmap for a short trip.
5. Learn when all of their senses are stimulated.
6. Learn best when they are active (i.e., when they discuss, influence, or participate).
7. Learn when they receive constructive feedback, be that feedback reflective or evaluative in nature.
8. Learn at their own pace. Again, the principle of individual differences is reinforced.

What has become very clear in these principles is that *how* the learner learns is at least as important as *what* the learner learns; in fact, how the learner learns determines how much is learned. This realization has had an enormous impact on our educational philosophy, practice, and assessment. It has also aided the concept of empowerment by pointing out yet again that the human being is not an automaton but a person who requires human consideration.

Another principle of adult learning theory is that learners learn best when they have the opportunity to participate in the learning process

— setting goals, defining the environment, and evaluating the results. Similarly, a manager who consults with employees about goals and work needs increases their commitment as well as enhances the outcome by bringing in more information relevant to a given project.

Much of what was once subsumed under the umbrella of adult learning theory has come to be called *experiential learning.* It was the basis of most laboratory education and T-group learning and is still directly influencing nearly all levels of formal and informal education. (Exhibit 1 elaborates on this concept.)

EXHIBIT 1.   What Is Experiential Education?

Definition

Experiential education is a cyclical process. After immediate concrete experiences, learners observe and reflect on their activities; their observations are brought together to form a "theory" from which new implications for their behavior are generated; these implications then serve as guides for learners as they practice new learning experiences.

Also called laboratory education

In laboratory learning, learners participate in and reflect on many kinds of activities; their principal concern is their own behavior — their "selves." The learning emphasis is on the "here-and-now" behaviors of participants.

Outcomes

Learners tend to "learn" the following from experiential education environments:

◆ Expanded consciousness of their world

◆ Recognition of choice in life's experiences

◆ A spirit of inquiry — a willingness to ask

◆ Authenticity, that is, realness in interpersonal relations

◆ A collaborative perception of authority relationships

Experiential education facilitator design skills

The role of facilitators is multifaceted. One of their key roles is to design laboratory learning. Five skills are of primary importance in order for effective experiential education to occur:

1. Ability to identify specific and explicit learning goals of the activity(ies)

EXHIBIT 1 *(continued)*.   What Is Experiential Education?

---

2. Sensitivity to and anticipation of participant responses and receptivity to the design

3. Ability to sequence learning activities

4. Ability to collaborate meaningfully and noncompetitively with other facilitators

5. Ability to modify and redirect the design while events are in progress

Experiential education learning components

There are five major components or activity types used in experiential education:

1. Intensive small groups

2. Structured learning experiences

3. Lecturettes/handouts (theory input)

4. Self-time

5. Back-home applications

As distinguished from traditional education

Traditional education focuses on processes meant to help plastic learners acquire the skills and information necessary to negotiate a fixed cultural environment.

Experiential education sees learning as a transaction between a fluid and unfixed learner and environment; each therefore undergoes change.

Reproduced by permission from J. Vogt et al., *Retaining Professional Nurses: A Planned Process,* p. 112. St. Louis, MO: C.V. Mosby, 1983.

A particularly useful perspective on experiential education is that of Kolb, Rubin, and McIntyre (1971), who conceptualize learning as a cyclical process of concrete experience, reflective observation, abstract conceptualization, and active experimentation. However, they note that different people learn differently, and each individual needs to learn in his or her own way. What makes this view especially important is its promise of a richer and more complete group-learning process. When people who have different learning strengths learn together, they not only learn more, but they gain an appreciation of the experience of others and of the benefits of reciprocity.

Once again the relevance of Kolb's conception for empowerment is self-evident. For the manager in particular it demonstrates the importance of valuing each person's capabilities and contributions and points to the synergistic benefits of helping people work together.

In 1982 Chris Argyris introduced his concept of double-loop learning. Simplistically stated, it reaffirms the idea that learning spirals out into larger and larger circles, if allowed to do so. Too often, however, childhood or work experiences impede full development of abilities. An empowering manager, by recognizing that people can learn in this fashion, not only can tap into the process but also can plan for it. He or she can ensure that the organization develops itself in such a way as to utilize the stronger human resources it will possess in the future.

The opportunity presented by the information explosion offers yet another way that adult (experiential) learning theory provides a base for empowerment. The need to deal effectively with the mounds of new information and use it to help us move forward has become imperative. The methodology and philosophical orientation of empowerment, combined with an educational framework of adult learning, can be the vehicle for organizational and personal success.

Organizational Structure

How organizations operate — what their structures look like, how organically integrated the parts of the structure are, and the process by which those structures are revised or maintained — directly affects each person, each subgroup, and the organization as a whole. (The interrelations among these three components are discussed later in this chapter.) Traditional organizational structure is either (1) a pre-existing structure, the organization's normal and unexamined way of operating or (2) some version of the hierarchical model of organization based on control and centralization. In 1964 Bradford, Gibb, and Benne stated that traditional organizations operate through:

1. Organizational structure/control (in place);
2. Goal determination (by top management);
3. Communication flow (via present channels);
4. Trust and acceptance (by employees).

They argue that this model is exactly upside down in terms of both the human condition and the most effective work structure. According to their own structure, known as the *trust theory,* people's first need is for acceptance and a sense of belonging. With membership in a group comes a sense of confidence that allows for fuller participation in the work process.

Once trust is in place, members can share data and make decisions in open and spontaneous ways; they are also free to gather and make use of relevant data from all sources. Such a group has a sense of its mission based on a broader reality, and each individual can more comfortably make his or her unique contribution. The identification of individual and group goals and the definition of productivity are clearer, and members can see the necessary interdependence of personal accomplishment and group achievement. At this point, a group is ready to organize or structure itself in the way that will best meet its goals. The data for this structuring process comes from both outside and within the group, from the competencies of the individual members, and from the specific goals at hand.

Gibb considered the relationship between person and work to be crucial to organizational and personal well-being. In 1969, the Dow Chemical Company conceptualized Gibb's work under the rubric of *participative technologies* and defined the outcomes if time and opportunity were given to work groups to move through these stages at an appropriate pace — one permitting critical issues to be resolved before moving to the next major concern. Exhibit 2 describes Dow's conception of such a work place. It is obvious that these "reactions to participative technologies" are virtually identical with the characteristics of empowered people and groups.

EXHIBIT 2. Reactions to Participative Technologies

Modal concern	Participative mode of entry	Modal reactions to participative technology (symptoms of resolved concerns)
Acceptance (membership)	Confidence Trust	Trust and acceptance of distrust Greater feeling of personal adequacy

EXHIBIT 2 (*continued*).   Reactions to Participative Technologies

Modal concern	Participative mode of entry	Modal reactions to participative technology (symptoms of resolved concerns)
		Acceptance of legitimate influence
		Positive effect toward members
		Diversity and nonconformity
		Acceptance of motive of others
		Easy expression of feeling and conflict
		Facade reduction
		Acceptance of idiosyncratic behavior
		Controls over processes, not people
Data (decision)	Openness Spontaneity Communication all directions	Clarity: minimization of defense
		Problem-solving behavior
		Trust, reduction of suspicion
		Increased feedback of suspicion
		Freedom of movement outside channels
		Reduction of intrapersonal disparities
		Open expression of feeling and conflict
		Increased permeability of boundaries
		Facade reduction

EXHIBIT 2 (*continued*).   Reactions to Participative Technologies

Modal concern	Participative mode of entry	Modal reactions to participative technology (symptoms of resolved concerns)
Goal (productivity)	Problem solving Freedom for self-assessment	Work orientation Visibility of intrinsic motivations Reduction of competitive behavior Creativity in sustained work Increased involvement in tasks Reduction of apathy Reduced need for work structure Diversity of behavior and attitudes Increasing congruence between work and play Reduced potency of extrinsic rewards Nonconformity High personal identity; ego strength
Control (organization)	Permissiveness Interdependence Freedom of form	Interdependence Diversity and nonconformity Fluidity of organization Greater unpredictability of behavior Reduced latent hostility Allocation of work by consensus or ability Reduction of symbolic fight Open expression of feeling and conflict

EXHIBIT 2 (*continued*).   Reactions to Participative Technologies

Modal concern	Participative mode of entry	Modal reactions to participative technology (symptoms of resolved concerns)
		Informality Spontaneity of form Reduced concern over organization form

This edited revision reprinted with permission of the Dow Chemical Company, Midland, Michigan, 1969.

In today's work world, there is much emphasis on project teams and on functional groups or departments. Structuring these groups in traditional ways will not be as effective as structuring them according to the human needs for acceptance, information, goals, and organization.

Systems Integration

The understandings derived from systems theory play a central role in the implementation, maintenance, and success of empowerment on the organizational level. Just as there are activities and strategies for empowering individuals and small groups, there are similar designs for organizations (see Galbraith, 1977; Likert, 1964; Mintzberg, 1983). Systems concepts like *decentralization, project/matrix relationships, participation,* and *multiple avenues of communications* have led to organizations that can respond quicker, be more creative, better utilize their human resources, and make sounder decisions — all leading to higher productivity.

The systems approach forces organizational leaders to recognize that (1) the sum is greater than the total of the parts and (2) what is good for one is likely to be good for all. It also demonstrates, however, that a change in one part of the system may not alter the whole system, even when its impact is felt throughout the organization. Even more important, a strategy for implementing and maintaining an empowered system focuses on all aspects of the system, not on just one or two (e.g., top management or labor relations).

The National Training Laboratories Institute (NTL) was a forerunner of the field of organization development (OD) in its development of both the theory and practice of interdependent systems. A 1968 NTL report defined the goals of OD as similar to those of laboratory learning and T-groups. Organization development "is, however, focused as much on the health of the organization as on the welfare and development of the individual" (Rogers, 1983, p. 136). The following list of objectives for a 1960s OD project recognizes the importance of system relations among people, work units, and the organization (NTL, 1968):[2]

1. To create an open, problem-solving climate throughout the organization;

2. To supplement the authority associated with role or status with the authority of knowledge and competence.;

3. To locate decision-making and problem-solving responsibilities as close to information sources as possible;

4. To build trust among individuals and groups throughout the organization;

5. To make competition more relevant to work goals and to maximize collaborative efforts;

6. To develop a reward system which recognizes both the achievement of the organization's mission (profits and service) and organization development (growth of people);

7. To increase the sense of "ownership" of organization objectives throughout the work force;

8. To help managers to manage according to relevant objectives rather than according to "past practices" or according to objectives which do not make sense for one's area of responsibility;

9. To increase self-control and self-direction for people within the organization.

The empowerment perspective has also borrowed from the *sociotechnical systems approach,* which originated in postwar Britain. This

---

[2] From "What Is OD?," 1968, *NTL Institute News and Reports,* Vol. 2, No. 3, pp. 1–2. Copyright 1968 by NTL Institute for Applied Behavioral Science. Reprinted by permission.

approach, which emphasized the careful matching of new technological work systems with pre-existing cultural (people) traditions in an organization, set the stage for more "human" organizations as well as higher levels of performance. Empowerment has its roots in the dual concern for better human environment and enhanced organizational performance.

CONCLUSION

Although empowerment has its roots in the foregoing fields and areas of research, its synthesis of these sources makes it a new and innovative construct. This account demonstrates that the theoretical and practical foundations are already in place. Having some sense of what has been considered and put into operation in the past can help us creatively visualize the future. Exactly where empowerment will allow organizations and individuals to venture is as yet unknown. Knowing where we have been and having the security of a conceptual field can help us more accurately define and assess the concept of empowerment and its usefulness for organizations.

Chapter 5 looks more closely at the interactions among the six conceptual roots the authors have discussed in the context of several models of empowerment and the field of organization development.

CHAPTER **5**

FRAMEWORKS FOR EMPOWERMENT

❖ *Overview*

An adequate framework for empowerment must consider both empow-ered and empowering behavior. Chapter 5 first presents the views of Kanter, Murrell, and Thomas and Velthouse on this core issue. The chapter then explores the discipline of organization development (OD), in particular its development of methods to "allow" individuals in or-ganizations to achieve their full potential. The chapter concludes with a description of a process model of empowerment that can guide both managers and organizations as they strive to incorporate empowering strategies into their daily activities.

As the foregoing chapters have demonstrated, defining the concept of empowerment is not an easy task. One aspect of empowerment is con-cerned with creating power for oneself (being *empowered*), and an-other concerned with helping others grow toward a state of empower-ment (being *empowering.*) Managers and organizations are addressing the issue of how they can create and maintain circumstances that em-power their employees. Yet another aspect considers the behavior of an empowered person as well as how the empowering person or setting affects others. Also central to the concept of empowerment is the inter-action among all the variables that affect empowerment (see Figure 3).

FIGURE 3.   Elements of Empowerment

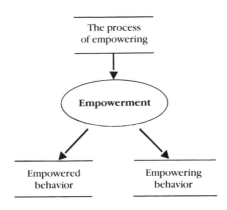

WHAT IS EMPOWERMENT?

A number of writers have recently explored the process of empowerment in organizations in ways that focus on both being empowered and being empowering. For Rosabeth Moss Kanter (1977), empowerment means giving power to people who operate at a disadvantage in the organization. She thus conceives of a continuum from powerless to empowered and encourages organizations to help people move toward the empowered end. Such organizations, she argues, "would reduce the dysfunctional consequences of powerlessness: low morale, bureaucratic rules-mindedness, and tight territorial control. They would benefit from speedy decisions and ability to take advantage of innovations. And they would develop better leaders, even among members of groups who have not traditionally become organizational leaders" (p. 281).

For organizations to empower their people, however, they must modify their formal structures. Empowerment, Kanter believes, must begin with fundamental structural modifications.

Dovetailing with Kanter's perceived relationship between structure and power is Ken Murrell's early perspective (1977) that empowerment "is an act of building, developing, and increasing power." Socialized power (empowered behavior) means that one has the "ability to influence" one's own reality. Consistent with his belief that power is not zero-sum based, Murrell identifies two major categories of empowerment: (1) self-empowerment, the ability to empower oneself, and (2) interactive empowerment, the process of creating power with others. The Murrell-Armstrong Empowerment Matrix (Murrell, 1985) identifies five settings of interactive empowerment (dyad, small group, organization, community, and society) and six empowerment methods (education, leading, mentoring/supporting, providing, structuring, and actualizing). These six methods, which provide an excellent framework for understanding how and when to initiate specific empowerment activities, serve as guides for a metaphorical tour through a gallery of empowerment in Chapter 6.

Kenneth Thomas and Betty Velthouse (1985) have taken another significant step toward conceptualizing the interaction between fundamental human needs and the system necessary to an empowering strategy. They identify three categories of human existence that are relevant to empowerment: belief systems, assessments, and enactment processes (see Figure 4). First, they argue, people's belief systems, or world views, and their self-concepts must not only allow empowering methods to affect behavior but must be in tune with the goals and methods of empowerment itself. Second, they identify four key assessments that individuals use to define their relationships with the environment:

1. *Impact* — Am I making a difference?
2. *Ability* — Do I have the competencies?
3. *Meaning* — Am I making a significant contribution?
4. *Progress* — Am I making headway? (Am I growing?)

FIGURE 4. Foundations for Empowered Behavior

Belief systems	Key assessments	Enhancement processes
World view	Impact	Attributing
Self-concept	Ability	Evaluating
	Meaning	Envisioning
	Progress	

The third category, enactment processes, delineates the means individuals use to translate their assessments into behavior:

1. *Attributing* — identifying reasons for successes or setbacks;
2. *Evaluating* — determining, in ways that are functional to the person's well-being, the pluses and minuses of alternative actions;
3. *Envisioning* — creating a clear and vivid mental image of success.

Assuming that one's belief systems, key assessments, and enactment processes are in harmony, high levels of activity, concentration, initiative, flexibility, and resiliency can be expected. These behaviors are, of course, empowering for the individual's quality of life and affect his or her self-concept and world view positively, thus providing a feedback loop and producing yet more harmony and higher levels of functioning.

Moreover, these behaviors are relevant to the person-organization relationship; they suggest that organizations can, in fact, develop "the power of confident people, passionately committed to meaningful goals, acting in accordance with their own higher values, taking risks and demonstrating initiative and creativity in the service of these goals" (Thomas & Velthouse, 1985, p. 1). Organizations can change how an individual is empowered by effecting directional changes in both key assessments and enactment processes. Such empowerment strategies, however, need to be systematic and tailored to each individual. The Thomas and Velthouse model not only provides a sound theoretical framework for defining and assessing empowerment but also demonstrates practically that "changes in empowerment are clearly possible through leadership, organization culture, job and organizational design, training, and other organizational processes and conditions" (p. 17).

THE OD-EMPOWERMENT RELATIONSHIP

The field of organization development (OD) was born out of 1960s attempts to free the individual to develop his or her fullest potential in group settings, growth-oriented counseling, and laboratory learning situations. Later, an organizational focus was developed, with an emphasis on team building, process consultation, and survey feedback methodologies. More recently, OD has generated hundreds of developmental strategies for affecting organizational design and corporate culture. In doing so it has made us more aware of the human values implicit in the growth process, as noted by Leland Bradford, Robert Tannenbaum, and others. Tannenbaum asserts that OD is characterized, among other things, by the possibility of the *unfolding* of individuals and systems. The concept of unfolding can be seen as parallel with *empowerment;* and the question of how to help systems unfold in useful, meaningful, helpful, value-based ways is similar to asking how we can help systems become empowering.

In the past fifteen years the field of OD has examined many of the issues related to empowerment, and it has produced many creative ideas and methods for mutually enhancing individuals and organizations. Perhaps most significant is its insight that the *process* orientation is more important than any given outcome. Organization development has contributed to the theory and practice of empowerment by providing a process, a value system, and a track record of accomplishment. If one can say that OD is empowering, then its three integral characteristics — being value based, process oriented, and successful in effecting changes in the leadership function — are also the basis of empowerment.

Over the years, OD has struggled with the issue of social ethics as well as with the question of personal well-being. And empowerment, like other change strategies, presents certain ethical dilemmas. Much of the enhancement of the work world attempted in the last thirty years has assumed that people who change will be better off at higher levels of self-actualization, but even this proposition must be rigorously examined. Like OD, empowerment must attend to both the *personal* dimension of empowering activity affecting individuals and the *philosophical* dialog about the ethics of change rooted in an assumption of the worth of each individual human being.

So what, after all, *is* empowerment? The answer to this question is multi-dimensional; it is also unfinished. What emerges at the core of empowerment is the creative individual. Regardless of the way in which this new model of leadership develops, it must recognize the self and the values of human freedom as its starting points. It must provide individuals with a sense of opportunity to affect themselves in positive ways. That alone would be sufficient. If, however, it also has implications for organizational life, then its root assumption is that this "affected self" will increase the organization's well-being. Using the model of *self-plus-empowerment,* we may eventually define a model of *organization-plus-empowerment* in which the processes and outcomes are congruent with a systems view.

A description of the empowered person based on the work of Thomas and Velthouse (1985) may be a description of the person of tomorrow. Such a person

> has an open and healthy worldview and a positive and accurate self-concept; sees self as making an impact, having the ability to do, recognizing meaning in one's pursuits, and progressing in life; is able to discern reasons for outcomes and to evaluate self in ways which are encouraging; and finally, that person is able to envision success, She or he is capable of meaningful activity, concentrated efforts, initiating action, flexible interactions, and personal resiliency. (p. 17)

A PROCESS MODEL OF EMPOWERMENT

Although empowerment has been previously defined as "giving power to," "creating power within," and "enabling," it is a long way from having a definitive meaning. It does, however, provide a new direction for our efforts on behalf of people. We have seen that empowerment has a very personal application, as in, "How am I empowered?" or "How can I help empower you?" It also has a systems or organizational application: "How do we empower employees, divisions, organizations, or other systems?" and "How do I as a manager empower others?"

The discussion of theoretical antecedents in this and the preceding chapter have pointed to a complex relationship, a pathway from the self to organizational well-being (see Figure 5). A central component of this process is commitment. The self is empowered through trust, commu-

FIGURE 5.   Process Model of Empowerment

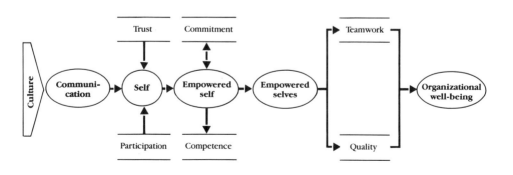

nication, and participation, which, in turn, bring about commitment (to people, institutions, projects, experiences). And commitment, in turn, connects the individual with others and with a sense of personal worth that brings a sense of self-fulfillment.

In an empowered organization, as illustrated by Figure 5, committed *individuals* contribute their expertise, often working together as *teams* to produce their best work on behalf of their own development and the integrity and growth of the *system*. To operationalize the linkages among these three levels of empowerment, top management must have a philosophical and applied commitment to the value of each individual and to the process of empowerment itself. All managers must consistently operate in ways that integrate and demonstrate this commitment.

This process model recognizes that a culture valuing openness, individual contributions, interdependence, and personal well-being must first be in place. Within it, a *communications process* that is multileveled, is honest, is open to asking and listening, and encourages everyone's input is crucial. Such a communications system (face to face or system wide) creates the opportunity for each person to express his or her authentic self and to receive feedback that fosters growth and promotes participation. This communications chain from the individual self, to trust, and to participation is almost an independent subsystem that must itself be carefully tended to maintain a state of personal empowerment.

Once the freedom of empowerment is attained, the individual feels an integral part of the system and becomes willing to commit himself or herself to group and organizational goals. In such settings interpersonal and group skills, as well as technical expertise and the valuation of each person's contribution, will produce teamwork, quality outcomes, and organizational well-being. Such well-being might be defined in numerous ways, but the most useful definitions will include not just the traditional criteria of productivity and profitability but also the kind of human and ethical values that lead to personal and organizational enhancement.

CHAPTER **6**

PICTURES OF EMPOWERMENT

 Overview

Building on the theoretical foundations and frameworks for empowerment discussed in Chapters 4 and 5, Chapter 6 begins the process of describing empowerment in managerial and organizational terms. It first identifies six categories of empowering behavior: educating, leading, mentoring/supporting, providing, structuring, and actualizing. A brief theoretical discussion of the role of empowerment in creating energy for personal and organizational development follows. Then, using the metaphor of the art gallery, the chapter tours the managerial and organizational floors of the gallery to view numerous pictures of empowerment. The chapter concludes with a focus on the effective group as perhaps the most important vehicle of an organization's long-range ability to become empowered and remain empowering.

THE ART GALLERY: SETTING AND FORM

This chapter presents pictures of empowerment. Many pictures are offered, pictures that in their complexity transcend simple prescriptions of how to be empowered or empowering. Some of the images may attract you; others may not. But even those that appear to offer little at first glance may warrant a second look from a new perspective. The theoretical antecedents of empowerment discussed in Chapter 4 are important to understanding its historical context; but, although that context frames the picture and hangs it, it does not capture the essence of the art of empowerment. This exhibition is the authors' effort to communicate what they feel is the essence of empowerment in action. They hope their efforts can place a mirror in front of managerial and top-management activities and provide readers with additional insights into the many different forms empowerment can take.

The deeper meaning of empowerment involves a creative act that frees a person, a group, an organization, even a total society, to behave in new ways. Empowerment provides options, degrees of freedom not allowed before. It creates and is created by the concept Argyris (1982) calls double-loop learning. In the first loop, empowerment breaks the frame that holds thinking in one groove and asks us to look fully and consciously at our current actions and how they are affecting us. But double-loop learning is not simply breaking free to see or feel something differently; it is also, in the second loop, taking the responsibility to stay attuned to the results of new behaviors and processes and to cooperate with others in their further development. The single-loop action is less an action than a reaction; to help empower others without also helping them see the consequences of their power is, in reality, not to be empowering at all.

So in looking at the pictures presented here, readers should consider how these empowering processes might affect them and their organizations. On the first floor are pictures of empowering methods focused on individual managers. The second floor of the exhibition contains pictures of organizational empowerment. On both floors pictures are arranged in "rooms" that relate to the general forms and specific actions empowerment can take: educating, leading, mentoring/supporting, providing, structuring, and actualization.

The process of *educating* as an empowerment act takes advantage of Francis Bacon's assertion that information is power; providing information to others is thus an empowering act. Moreover, except in a zero-sum political world, education is as beneficial to the manager and the organization as it is to the individual, for well-informed people create a more accurate picture of the situation and can make better business decisions. Educating, of course, goes beyond simple information sharing. It also implies helping others learn to use and effectively create further, more useful information, with all the resulting advantages to the organization.

The second form of empowerment is effective *leading.* Leadership that excites, energizes, motivates, and liberates others is the essence of empowerment. Leaders whose ego strength allows them to empower others to exceed even their own records help the organization benefit from everyone's talents.

Mentoring/supporting actions can also help build another's competence and self-confidence. This form of empowering is generally more personal and is based on a closer emotional attachment than leading. The person who serves as a mentor can also gain increased power from seeing others do well and from providing a model of success for the organization. When members of an organization play the mentor role for one another the net result is likely to be increased power for the system as a whole.

The fourth form of empowering, called *providing,* is very often overlooked. Providing is finding and supplying others with the resources necessary for their success. To empower a carpenter, one must provide the best tools; to empower a computer specialist, one must provide the latest in hardware and software. Of course, it is not always possible to have the best and latest of everything; but it is clear that a company that invests money in limousines for its executives instead of in the best tools for its employees has chosen not to empower its workers. A capable person — even one with an education, good leadership, support, and the power to create a good product or service — is limited by the resources available.

The fifth form of empowerment to be pictured, *structuring,* is probably the most complicated to explain. A person is only as powerful as the structure will allow him or her to be. All the participative management in the world will not produce an empowered organization unless the structure also allows for it. In the United States, for example, the Constitution provides a structure of empowerment for the political system. Although it may have faults, it can be improved through amendment (a double-loop process). *Structuring* primarily pertains to organizational arrangements and procedures, but it can also pertain to an individual's job or work life. Job descriptions and specifications can be empowering structures if they represent a good fit between the person and position and if they allow for growth and development in terms of new and creative ways of empowering.

The final form of empowering builds on all five of the previous forms, which come together as the *actualized* spirit in which the individual performs at a high level the work he or she is best prepared to do. Such a self-actualizing process is a joint responsibility of person and organization and is geared not toward perfection but toward psychological health. A person who feels right about his or her work most of the time produces more work of higher quality. Although the five previous forms of empowerment can help create a self-actualized state, the final responsibility must always rest with the individual. As a collective entity, an organization needs actualized members to build the actualized culture that creates an empowered organization able to compete on a global scale.

These six forms and the pictures reflective of each are only parts of the story, for empowerment is a process of growth and not a final goal to be achieved. It is a pathway, a way of being. A few of the interesting sites along this path can be seen during an excursion through an art gallery of empowerment pictures and can perhaps start leaders along their own paths of empowerment.

CREATING ENERGY FOR DEVELOPMENT

Before beginning the tour, the reader should be aware of one further characteristic of empowerment. So far, discussions of the concept have recognized it as a process that creates *power*. Yet another product of empowerment is *energy*, in particular the sort of energy necessary to support, reinforce, and encourage individual and organizational development. In algebraic terms, this concept might be expressed as

$$E = (En)D \rightarrow P$$

where empowerment (E) is energy (En) that multiplies when it is developmental (D) in nature; the greater the developmental energy, the greater the power (P). Moving mentally through this art gallery of empowerment, readers will be able to imagine how they or their groups, systems, or societies might behave or what everyone might become if such energy were to become available.

MANAGERIAL CHARACTERISTICS OF EMPOWERMENT

Florence Nightingale (1820–1910), in describing her profession, avowed that: "Nursing is an art; and if it is to be made an art, it requires as exclusive a devotion, as hard a preparation, as any painter's work." A similar effort is needed to conceive and implement empowerment, as the following pictures of managerial strategies for creating energy and, thus, power demonstrate. The pictures are composite images of how various forms of an empowering managerial style can both create an environment for healthy human beings and stimulate successful performance.

❖ **Case Vignette 7.**   *Educating*

> Ed Coti was recently hired by a division of X-tec Corporation to improve the support that the computer services unit provided line managers by instituting a new materials management program. In his first week on the job Ed saw a dedicated crew of professional computer experts, the most senior of whom had only been at X-tec two years. Although he knew high turnover rates were normal in this technical area, he also realized that such rates represented considerable hidden costs.
>
> One of Ed's first methods for empowering people was to provide them with information about X-tec's position in a competitive business environment, about management's goals for the company, and about the effect of these external and internal factors on everyone in his group. In a second effort he initiated a process for members of the group to design a framework of services they would provide to users. To do so, he first invited users and other key actors inside and outside the organization to brief the group on what they needed from the support group to meet corporate goals. He also made a point of educating the visitors about the strengths, limits, and needs of the group and encouraged them to share helpful information. He did not always speak of this as an empowerment philosophy, but when he sensed a receptivity to discuss information as power he negotiated agreements for individuals to empower one another by sharing information.
>
> Ed's boss encouraged him to proceed in this manner. In fact, even before he took the job Ed had educated himself about how X-tec used information; he talked to people inside the corporation, several customers, and a friend who had recently been a consultant to X-tec. In addition to educating the group and initiating improved communication with users, Ed worked with his boss and the other managers to establish agreements about information sharing and to promote his view that it was the key to success for both these managers and the corporation.

❖ *Case* **Vignette 8.**   *Leading*

Edi Ling came to First Northeast Bank from San Francisco and immediately felt the cultural differences between the coasts. She was hired by First because her predecessor had worked himself to the point of collapse, trying to carry a division with a reputation for mediocre performance. What Edi experienced on her first visit confirmed the reputation; but when she reviewed the files of the fifteen people in the group, she was impressed with their potential. In pre-employment discussions with her new boss, she made it clear that her style of leadership was based on maximum delegation and dedication to developing people to do more and better than they had ever done before. She compared herself to a coach: the people in her division would play the game, and she would do everything she could to make sure they had all the power needed to perform. She would nurture a sense of mutual responsibility and a commitment to helping the company achieve its goals.

Because this was a drastic change from the past leadership style, it took some time to reach agreement with her boss and the team. Her strategy would not work, she repeatedly said, unless her boss trusted her, she trusted the people in the division, and they trusted the process. Inevitably, there were questions, and on more than one occasion she felt she was being tested. Some of the tests involved desperate ploys to get her to rescue people she knew did not need saving. On these occasions she put the issue on the table with the people involved, discussed what had occurred, and reached agreement about what they would expect of one another in similar situations. Edi's success at using leading as an empowering strategy became apparent when one of her assistants was promoted to a position higher than her own and several others were recruited by other divisions of the company.

Like Ed, Edi had made sure of her boss's support before accepting the position; and her contract ensured that her own success would be measured by how well her people performed for the company. Her own career path was being set out as a combination line manager and human resource development expert. The organization benefited in many ways from Edi's leadership style; most importantly, the people working with her felt a renewed and clearly rewarded sense of competence and confidence. A few people referred to her empowering style, but most simply respected her for helping turn a group of mediocre performers into a high-performing team whose members were recognized for their contributions.

Pictures of empowerment can be found that are quite old as well as young and fresh.

❖ Case Vignette 9.   *Mentoring/Supporting*

The odd couple in MGB's organization was the team of sixty-year-old George Toring and thirty-year-old Nancy Porting, representing opposite ends of the electrical engineering field. One was a recent master's degree graduate from the highest tech end of the engineering spectrum, and the other a thirty-year veteran who had studied electrical engineering under the G.I. Bill in the late 1940s.

George's life-long contribution to MGB lay in his commitment to finding and developing young and talented colleagues to help the firm move into the twenty-first century. Some of his protégés were now several rungs above him on the organizational ladder and remained his strongest supporters. His support of Nancy Porting was only one more example of his heartfelt conviction that people will do well if they get the right information and the opportunity to do well. Since MGB had a fine reputation in the field, it attracted good people, and George could take engineering skills for granted. He focused his efforts on helping protégés make sense of the organization and identify people who could be depended on to get the job done. Even though the terms *network* and *high-performing system* were only jargon to George, he had learned the reality behind them through many years of practice and experience.

Nancy Porting was the oldest child in a family of five and had learned early the pleasures of supporting others and watching them grow. Her parents had inspired her to try for an engineering scholarship, which she won. Thanks to the support of her family, friends, and teachers, she went on to become one of the highest-ranking graduates of a very demanding engineering program in a noted southern university.

A few management courses had helped her see the managerial role in terms of providing others with support and encouragement. At MGB her success in empowering others was soon noticed, and upper management decided to give her supervisory responsibilities. Her reputation as a fast-track young professional who developed people as well as herself and the backing of her mentor, George Toring, won her support at all levels in the company.

Although thirty years in age separated these two managers, their styles were congruent; and the results proved beneficial to the organization. Their division exceeded the human resource development goals they had set for themselves, and the work performance of the division was exemplary. The new MGB management, which was studying strategies for creating an empowering organizational culture, often focused its attention on the Toring/Porting division.

———————————————————————————————————

 Case Vignette 10.   *Providing*

For six years, Vic Rovid had been manager of information services for ET AL Inc., a giant Chicago-based conglomerate. Each year since he had been promoted into management from his technical position, he had played the budget game according to the rules, written and unwritten. And every year the results were identical: Vic received a total budget increase of 6 percent. In fact, throughout the company most increases in operating budgets were within this same range, even though both the company and its external environment had recently undergone considerable change. The company had fallen into the routine of allocating its year's budget based on last year's usage; and, of course, no unit ever failed to spend all of its budget.

Every year, Vic prepared the case to support his arguments that the company would have to automate its internal information systems or suffer the consequences of an increasingly inefficient system. In doing this homework each year, Vic became quite an expert on the new information technologies. After experiencing one more year of a frustrating budget process, Vic learned that a rival company was looking for a person with his background.

When he interviewed with the firm, he experienced a much more open and progressive environment in which budget decisions were tied to performance projections and needs. Nonetheless, before accepting the offer of a management position similar to his own job at ET AL, he sat down and calculated a salary increase and a budget he would insist on having. The company responded by accepting his salary request and proposing a meeting in which he was to explain what he would deliver if given this budget. Never before had he had the chance to present his plans and to justify a budget to bring them to fruition; as his excitement mounted he felt the energy and power that flowed from this responsibility. The negotiations were not easy, but finally a figure was agreed on that Vic felt would meet the department's needs and challenges. Vic accepted the job offer.

Working with others who also felt excited about their jobs because they too had adequate resources, Vic felt empowered. He used this personal lesson on empowerment by helping his own people plan the next year's budget based on the goals and aspirations they set for themselves. By linking resources with performance, he was able to see how much more people were capable of achieving when they had adequate resources.

Moreover, although Vic's own managerial responsibilities were over a staff function, he sought support from the line managers by finding out how the department could help them achieve their goals. Thus Vic not only empowered himself and those in his department by getting them the resources they needed to do their jobs, but also ensured that their work would be valued by line managers. The payoff, in the following year's budget, was a more than incremental increase.

In Vic's old company, management just could not handle the conflict and complexity that might arise from making resource allocation decisions on anything but a "fair," across-the-board basis. This conservative avoidance of conflict was only one of six reasons (the absence of the six empowerment methods) that Vic's old company filed for corporate reorganization the next year and several of his former subordinates called him about job possibilities.

❖ ───

The decision to provide people with the resources they need to get the job done is not always the most efficient, economic decision in a static world. But in a dynamic, ever more demanding environment, it is often the only choice of action. When motivation is low and a simple tool or piece of equipment is not available, it is easy to take the rest of the day off. But when a little extra resource is available, a worker's performance might also reflect that little extra.

 Case Vignette 11. *Structuring*

Steve Truct, of Standard Research Group (SRG), has been in personnel work now for ten years; and each year he feels he has learned more about his company. Steve's first few years at SRG were very frustrating as he was moved in and out of three different personnel positions. SRG's policy was to test new people in at least three different jobs before identifying the "right" places for them. Steve concluded that this practice was responsible for the company's 36-percent turnover rate among young professionals. He believed it would have to change this policy in order to retain the young professionals needed in the future.

Steve's approach to effecting this change was first to document his own successes in reducing staff turnover and then to find better ways of managing people. In his own department Steve instituted a program of helping fit the person to the job based on the latest research in this area. Before implementing it he discussed the strategy with his staff members and obtained their thinking on how best to proceed. In any given year there were several open positions on Steve's staff of twenty-three. For the first three years of his new strategy, the turnover rate in the department dropped below 10 percent. Steve calculated that the overall corporate rate of 36 percent cost SRG approximately $2.7 million in direct and indirect costs, even without including the cost of lost production and low morale.

Steve's proposals to help structure more effective procedures for establishing a fit between person and job centered around empowering members of work groups to become more involved in structuring their jobs and deciding whom to hire in the department. The top managers' need for a sense of control was transcended by asking *them* to serve as sounding boards to which lower-level groups would have to explain their hiring decisions in accordance with both fit and an agreed-on set of performance indicators. Within two years, SRG's turnover rate had been halved at a significant cost savings. Just as important, work teams were feeling that they had some control over their own destinies, and new hires were starting out in jobs that seemed to relate to both their skills and interests. Moreover, Steve had structured a higher-level job for himself as policy review specialist, a position in which he worked with top managers to help them discover additional ways SRG could empower its employees, take better advantage of the human potential that existed, and cut unnecessary costs.

Case Vignette 12.   *Self-Actualizing*

Through all of her 23 years of life, Aliz had been surrounded by people who wanted her to have all the best in terms of opportunities and freedom. She had attended schools carefully selected by her parents to foster her unique development. In her excellent high school she took on with excitement all the advanced courses designed for gifted children. Aliz received offers of merit scholarships from many fine universities and chose the one she felt offered her the most freedom and the best opportunity for close faculty involvement. After college she attended the MBA program at a nearby major metropolitan university.

After interviewing with a number of companies, Aliz finally accepted a position, at a salary several thousand dollars less than she was offered elsewhere. She was convinced that her employer, New Systems Research (NSR), offered her several important advantages. First, she sensed, and later confirmed with friends and associates, that NSR insisted on information sharing and a no-secrets policy. Second, she was able to identify managers who were interested in her capabilities and who were doing technical and managerial work she respected. Third, when a senior executive agreed to discuss NSR's mentorship program, he also suggested that she talk to others about how well the program worked for them. Fourth, the facilities and equipment she needed to function effectively were available and state of the art; and the company was committed to keeping them updated. Finally, NSR had evolved into a network structure of organizational relationships; and the job she was offered had been defined by the members of the team she would be joining. The position was a good fit with her own background and interests and was an integral part of the company's five-year development plan.

Aliz felt she could find her professional self in such a setting. But what made her choice easy was that it appeared important to her future colleagues that she feel comfortable asking for their help and support in finding her full human potential as part of NSR. They easily disclosed their own life stories and feelings about NSR, and Aliz felt a mutual empathy with them and identified strongly with the core values on which NSR based its everyday activities.

The demands of the job were challenging, and the collegial relationships, though very supportive, demanded a sense of shared responsibility to maintain and develop NSR's founding principles. Aliz felt confident that she would be able to contribute and grow at NSR and that no employee's achievements would be overshadowed by those of a few; everyone would receive his or her share of credit for the company's success. Something different was occurring at NSR, something that she was sure offered her, as a beginning professional, an exciting career path. She picked up that sense of excitement from others; and, although a few of the long-term employees tried to describe to her the spirit of NSR, they ended up admitting that words could not adequately describe the atmosphere.

 ──

The spirit of an empowered person or an actualized organization is not always easy to describe. It is perhaps best understood from a feeling and not an analytical perspective. We do know that actualization, the final form of empowerment, comes from the coexistence and mutual support of all the other forms. Although hard to put into words, it is something we can work to bring about. And, when it occurs, we can build it into our organizations' very being, as the pictures on the second floor of the gallery demonstrate.

ORGANIZATIONAL CHARACTERISTICS OF EMPOWERMENT

A tour of the second floor of the art gallery reveals pictures that go beyond what individual managers can do to the steps organizations can — and do — take toward empowerment. In the organizations pictured — or in some cases, only sketched hypothetically — experimentation and a trust of the empowerment process have already yielded significant payoffs. By developing the same six categories of empowering behavior employed by empowering managers, the organizations pictured here are attracting and holding the best people; and they are competing success-fully in world markets precisely because they take full advantage of their valuable human resources. Because of their responsiveness and flexibil-ity, they can jump on an opportunity and pursue it as if their very exis-tence depends on it, which it often does. These are the organizations described by Vaill (1982) as high-performing systems and by Peters and Waterman (1982) as models of excellence. They are empowered com-panies that have empowering managers and that are made up of empow-ered people who believe they can make a difference.

❖ **Case Vignette 13.**   *Educating*

GDS faces increasing competition and is losing its exclusive control of a declining market; the company's pace of change has not kept up with a changing world. It must either respond to a dynamic marketplace or sur-render its long-held industry leadership.

What does it do? It commits itself to a major program of human re-source development, budgeting $8 million annually to personnel devel-opment, especially management education. Even though the figure seems high, per capita expenditures on training are much less than those of many other firms. GDS's educational philosophy combines knowledge acquisition and skill development into an integrated approach, with line managers establishing development and training goals for their own departments. It teaches chemists about organizational change strategies and janitors about reading and basic English fluency; it trains secretaries as *developers* of other secretaries and as *consultants* to help develop more effective work teams. In short, GDS uses education as an empowerment strategy.

Any modern corporation that, like GDS, faces a competitive environment must first examine itself to discover its comparative advantages. In the United States low labor rates and an abundance of workers willing to do just about anything are *not* advantages. Nor is the culture a homogeneous one with a docile and obedient population. The United States is a dynamic and energetic society, full of diversity and conflict; it is a society of change that values *both* independence and teamwork. In such a dynamic and diverse society, education and the sharing of information about world needs can fuel an empowerment process. Large firms committed to educating their people have already come part way along the road to empowerment.

The pictures in the next room of the gallery are only sketches. Although innovative and risk-taking firms are still the exception, as the pace of change quickens organizations that thrive on crisis will emerge as the leaders (Peters & Waterman, 1982).

❖ **Case Vignette 14.**   *Leading*

Leadership in the successful firms of tomorrow will not be limited to a few people high in the hierarchy but will be found in numerous pockets of excellence and in successful teams throughout the organization. Entrepreneurship *within* large organizational settings (as initiated structurally and philosophically by Gulf Oil in the mid-1980s) will be widespread.

The large firm of tomorrow may be a multinational enterprise with no identifiable country of origin — not a monolithic giant but a loosely coupled network of separate divisions, each competing for its own ever-changing market. The parent company will serve as a secure base for branching out into new areas, like a space station launching ships toward the stars. Already some large organizations that lead in their own fields have shown no hesitancy to enter new fields. RCA and Westinghouse have both created divisions for selling in the international arena services that have little to do with the electrical industry. They have used the leadership and expertise of their staff people, developed in their industry, to market a service on a global basis. Other large American firms have expanded both vertically and horizontally, using America's comparative advantage to market high-tech products and services internationally.

The key to such broadening strategies is the discovery and nurturance of new leadership. Creating new leaders to pursue new markets on a global level demands an empowerment perspective. Operating in fifty different countries will tax the hierarchically structured organizations beyond their capacity to bear; the hopelessly large bureaucracies some have labeled "corpocracies" will not survive. New organizational forms and new leadership styles are being created daily: profit centers, autonomous work teams, and "adhocracies" are only three examples of alternative organizational forms of leadership.

A few organizations that recognize the role of the mentoring function in preparing professionals have instituted formal programs of matching mentor and protege.

❖ **Case Vignette 15.** *Mentoring/Supporting*

Many law firms and other professional associate-based organizations have institutionalized the support climate necessary for organizational empowerment. In addition to professional mentorship programs, new models of effective apprenticeship are setting the stage for empowering a new generation of workers and leaders in which the two roles may eventually merge.

Moreover, organizations using mentoring strategies to prepare their next generations of leadership are expanding this concern for the individual. Some are implementing a more broadly based set of supporting policies involving career-development contracts and commitments to invest in individualized development programs at all levels.

As the "baby boom" labor force ages and the economy develops, the scarcity of young professionals will require even more carefully designed programs to prevent increasing the distance between levels of the organization. This scarcity and the new market realities will add to the pressure for fundamental organizational change in the direction of a "flattening" of hierarchies. Not providing this support will create a considerable social problem in our organizations, as well as our societies, producing a we/they and have/have not dichotomy when we need to be unified in facing external economic and other pressures. In the United States such a two-tiered society is already emerging. We can perhaps find an antidote to it in empowered organizations, using company-wide mentorship programs to make performance and not status the focus of reward.

In the late 1960s and early 1970s, General Foods (GF) received considerable attention for an experiment in empowerment that went by different labels — job enrichment, autonomous work teams, and sociotechnical systems. One of the key lessons in GF's successes was the necessity for *providing.*

❖ **Case Vignette 16.**   *Providing*

At the Topeka plant, GF's innovative facility, one of the major differences noted in the culture was the commitment to production felt by the workers (Murrell, 1976). This feeling, which resulted in production figures that exceeded engineering estimates of what was possible, came about for two reasons. First, the structure of the work teams helped workers feel empowered; second, they were provided with the resources necessary to achieve this high level of production. Several of the plant managers were willing to "rock the boat" and make demands on GF for the needed resources.

In the long run, however, this is a sad picture; the people who produced the most were not rewarded, and organizational empowerment stopped at the plant site. Internal problems caused the creative and empowering managers to leave GF (to do quite well elsewhere); and the workers were never rewarded, as they had been promised, for their extra efforts.

In this well-studied case, an organizational empowerment strategy of providing had established a sense of shared responsibility and had helped create an empowered work force. A new model for production operations and a flattened organizational hierarchy resulted in both a profitable operation and some very anxious middle managers who were resistant to change.

 Case Vignette 17. *Structuring*

Over the last twenty to thirty years, only a few organizations have departed radically from mainstream corporate organizational structure.

One of the more innovative and creative examples is a Washington-based firm originally known as International Group Plans or IGP. This company set out to create an organizational structure modeled on the United States Constitution. Its young and charismatic founding president, Jim Gibbons, wanted to harmonize his deeply held convictions about the greatness of our democratic experiment as a country with his responsibility as a founder and leader of a profit-making company. Jim read voraciously in the organizational sciences and democratic management literature and designed numerous structures to help IGP achieve its democratic goals. The firm became for many (e.g., Bernstein, 1976; Maccoby, 1977) the model of a democratic organization, a live laboratory of experimentation and innovation for studying the empowerment process.

IGP succeeded, failed, and learned at a furious pace. Participants loved or hated the experience — often at the same time. The energy that was created spawned new knowledge, confidence, and human connections. It managed (not controlled) its empowering energies through centers of responsibility where managers, called "center forwards," used information to make tactical and operational decisions, while democratically formed committees set out strategic goals and policies. The center forward (management) positions went through a validation process similar to an election to ensure that managers maintained the confidence and support of those with whom they worked. If they failed to do so, others could step forward to try to do better. All members of the organization could work on any of the committees (more actively if elected), and company ownership and profits were shared.

Midway through the experiment it became obvious that the company's success depended on training people in the skills needed to function in a democratic society. A full-time professional facilitated development of programs to prepare people for the significantly different levels of responsibility demanded by an empowered organization. As the role of the facilitator developed, it became the focal point of the democratic spirit and energies associated with an empowering setting. In this case, an actualized organization was evolving years before the formal concept of empowerment was created to support such efforts.

The pictures in the next room are really the culmination of our gallery tour, for the organizational characteristic they illustrate combines all those seen on the tour thus far.

Abraham Maslow used the term *self-actualization* to describe the state of psychological health in which a person strives for, and occasionally realizes, his or her true potential. This experience need not, however, be confined to the individual. This summit of human experience can offer challenges to organizations, on behalf of individual members *and* their own development. Although still rare, there are actualized organizations, and pictures of how they function are not difficult to create.

❖ **Case Vignette 18.** *Organizational Actualization*

An actualized organization is a healthy environment, where people feel empowered to be all they can be and where knowledge of both the internal workings and the external conditions are open and shared with everyone. The microcomputer sitting on each person's desk is a symbol of the openness and trust that is set as deeply into the organization's culture as the interconnected wiring of the networking system. An underlying belief in actualization is essential to providing the information that passes from desk to desk technologically and to creating the organizational spirit that propels the sharing of both information and feelings.

In this actualized organization, role models — throughout the organization and not just at its top (if a single top can be said to exist) — demonstrate empowering leadership. Making support available to all members of the organization is deeply imbedded in the actualized culture, and the formal mentorship process is designed to help the organization develop beyond its present potential. In addition, the organization actively encourages assorted self-help associations and support networks.

The budgets and purchasing policies of the organization are designed to help the company produce high-quality goods and services. This realization of the importance of quality is grounded in the economic realities of a competitive marketplace and is shared by all members, not just the proverbial "bean counters" who help control costs. The job of providing what is needed for everyone to do the best possible job is not a delegated responsibility; like leadership, the concern for quality and economy is found throughout the organization.

The actualization of a structure that demands not just participation but responsibility requires formal and informal methods of development and training of individuals and work groups. Commitment to human development goes well beyond the traditional human resource staff roles in use in many progressive corporations today. The concern and caring for others in a whole-life perspective is part of the values of this organization, which demand more from each person while offering more in return.

Concern for the future and its institutionalized method of self-evaluation (see Appendix) keep the company focused on preparing itself for the future.

These attributes of the actualized organization depend almost entirely on the ability of effective and mature work teams to establish and maintain this high level of organizational life.

THE EFFECTIVE GROUP AS THE VEHICLE FOR EMPOWERING ORGANIZATIONS

The transformational potential to help an organization empower and then actualize itself lies in the form of the effective group, the most likely vehicle of empowerment. The empowering process, combined with the maturing nature of organizational responsibility, will help the group establish the three basic competency foundations: trust, proactive skills, and clarity. The group developmental process allows, encourages, and supports both individual and organizational actualization.

First, the trust foundation is established and made visible in face-to-face group encounters. Because trust is a prerequisite for valid information sharing, the encounter sets the scene for stage two development. Proactive skills, operating at all levels of the organization, allow issues and problems about work and other organizational relationships to be expressed and dealt with. They cannot be resolved, however, unless the third foundation principle, clarity of purpose and role, is well developed. Thus, when trust is built, proactive skills can be developed and clarity of purpose and structure can result from the information that is shared. Clarity as a product of trust and information sharing also leads directly to the organization's eventual destination, which must be articulated and embodied in a strategic plan.

Groups also serve as primary links with other groups at all levels, whether above, below, or lateral. How well the groups in an organization network among themselves, recognizing their interdependence and building ways to enhance it, is a major determinant of organizational well-being. Insofar as it is successful in empowering and creating energy, the linking of individual and organization through the group becomes even more important. The process of empowerment of the organization through the group is explored in depth in the following chapter on action-empowerment.

The future is generally more fair to those prepared for it, and there are several ways in which to become better prepared. Organizations, as they prepare for the future, must widen their awareness of the options open to them. Each individual, too, must realize that an individual's freedom is dependent on the choices he or she is able to envision. The pictures in this chapter are meant to offer options and not a limited set of choices — a liberating sense of freedom, not a prescribed pathway.

CHAPTER 7

PARALLEL ACTION EMPOWERMENT: FROM SELF TO SYSTEM

❖ *Overview*

This chapter introduces and defines the concept of action empowerment, making explicit the parallels between the development of empowerment in the individual and in the system. It describes the ways both individuals and organizations become aware of the implications of empowerment for themselves and are gradually transformed into empowered, and empowering, leaders or organizations. Discussion of this parallel transition process includes an explanation of specific characteristics that individuals and organizations develop along the path to empowerment.

The foundations of empowerment presented in Chapters 4 and 5 and the case vignettes of Chapter 6 have pointed to several dimensions of this construct that are central to its meaning:

1. Empowerment means a growth, not a distribution, of power.
2. That growth of power is a dynamic, liberating force that frees energy to use or to generate more power.
3. Empowerment is facilitative in its nature and its implementation; it enables, allows, permits.

4. Empowerment is both a pragmatic and a realistic methodology, a process based on well-tried activities.

5. An organizational action can be recognized as successful empowerment if the organization accomplishes more than it did prior to the action and if its members value that action. An individual corollary can be drawn as well: an individual's sense of being empowered is discernible when an action leads to enhanced achievement of goals that he or she values highly.

6. Abilities shared with others can create a self-fulfilling drive for empowerment.

BECOMING EMPOWERED AND BEING EMPOWERING

As suggested in the discussion of the process model in Chapter 5, empowerment occurs through an empowering process. In the first step the manager becomes empowered; only when a manager has become empowered can he or she be empowering for others. The same is true for an organization: in the process of becoming an empowered system, the organization will emerge as an empowering entity. Two major implications arise from this understanding: (1) the process of *becoming* empowering is as important as being empowered; and (2) the process occurs in stages, much like the unfolding maturation of the individual described by Carl Rogers (1961) in *On Becoming a Person*.

The actions of empowerment described in this chapter illustrate this unfolding or developmental process at both the managerial and organizational levels. While the popular and research literature is rich in information about how to become an empowered and empowering individual, there is less specific information about how organizational empowerment is created.

For the manager and for human resource development professionals, action empowerment means contributing to the organization's development and creating actions that are mutually empowering for the system and its employees. The realization of interdependence — whether as a world society, functional manager, family member, or participant in a work team — makes finding empowering strategies that empower each entity while nurturing the various parts of the system the true challenge of empowerment.

PARALLEL ACTION EMPOWERMENT

Certain primary actions define for both the individual manager and the organization where to start and how to progress through their parallel processes of empowerment. This parallel conceptual framework can help identify the points of stress in the developmental process. For example, a manager may be at point Y on the empowerment pathway while his or her department may still be at point X; or a manager may be at point A when the organization has already progressed to point B. Having a way to visualize the process and describe the current state of empowerment of particular people and units can help the manager or the organization plan how to proceed.

Figure 6 illustrates what occurs within each of these separate processes as individuals, managers, units, departments, or divisions develop toward empowerment. Implicit in these parallel components of action empowerment is an awareness of the cultural environment and a model for change that goes far beyond the work place.

Self-Awareness

For each person, knowing the self is a lifelong task. Managers or individuals must know who they are, recognize their own changing characteristics, and be willing to evaluate their actions in the here-and-now (e.g., "Am I being empowering right now?"). For the manager, there are literally hundreds of personal development and assessment instruments and activities to heighten self-awareness — from questionnaires to counseling to weekend retreats to asking superiors and subordinates for feedback.

For an organization too the job of knowing itself is an ongoing process; it needs to develop a self-awareness similar to the individual's. It can do so through mission statements and various self-assessment strategies, organizational audits, climate surveys, and/or cultural diagnoses. (See Appendix for an example of such a diagnostic instrument.)

In neither case, of course, should such a self-evaluation be a one-time activity. To remain empowered and empowering, organizations and individuals must continually monitor themselves, preferably at set intervals — unless sudden changes warrant immediate reassessment.

FIGURE 6. Parallel Action Empowerment

Manager (Individual)	Ongoing assessment	Organization (Subsystem)
Self-awareness		Self-awareness
Growth orientation		Growth orientation
CLARITY ABOUT AND COMMITMENT TO EMPOWERMENT		
Interpersonal competency		Mature and open human interaction
Group leadership/ membership skills and technical expertise		Group productivity and product excellence
Ability to link self and groups to the system		Interdependence, linkages, and collaboration within a system
Ability to understand and interact with, relate to, contribute to one's environment	Change is constant	Awareness of external circumstances and a commitment to enhancing society positively

Growth Orientation

Every manager must learn that self-development is normal and that growth is inevitable. Organizations too must recognize that survival becomes more assured through growth and change. The psychological perspective that emerged from the motivation theories in the 1950s and 1960s suggests that human growth means taking risks and being proactive; those who shrink from life and those who merely react to it are not empowered or empowering.

In organizations an orientation toward growth is translated into four specific kinds of activities (see Exhibit 3.) First, such organizations develop and state their vision. Second, they recognize that development means education and learning; and they conduct training programs that recognize the personal, organizational, and task needs of the system. Third, they emphasize quality — in their operations and in their products or services. And, finally, they have a proactive norm, a bias toward taking action.

EXHIBIT 3.   Characteristics of Growth Orientation in an Organization

---

◆ A clear, current, relevant, and developmental vision
◆ Ongoing training and development that fosters competence and readiness for achievement
◆ A foundation of quality in all aspects of activity
◆ A proactive perspective in the fabric and operations of the organization

---

Clarity about and Commitment to Empowerment

The combination of a proactive norm and self-awareness prepares both managers and organizations to learn about empowerment. Individuals, units, and organizations must take the time to examine the concept thoroughly and to explore the fit between empowerment and themselves. Managers and organizations alike must decide separately whether they want to proceed along the empowerment path or travel by some other road. If they decide to proceed, however, there must be a well-articulated commitment to becoming and being empowered. Individuals in particular must recognize the need to change personal and managerial behaviors because empowerment is, for most, a life change rather than just a new managerial style.

When these changes occur in individuals and more and more members begin to make decisions and act in terms of empowerment, the cultural environment of an organization changes. As this culture of empowerment emerges, it becomes difficult and highly disruptive to attempt to return to the past. Once individuals have committed themselves to empowerment, the organization must set out policies and structural guidelines to support their empowerment behaviors.

Interpersonal Competency; Mature and Open Interactions

Each individual and manager must carefully hone his or her interpersonal skills, for these most fundamental of empowerment capabilities translate commitment to action. Especially important are the abilities to listen and reflect, to describe, to give and receive feedback, to confront and disagree, to support and encourage. These face-to-face skills, along with strong writing ability, will convey the manager's commitment to empowering his or her staff members.

The organization too must learn to reinforce mature and open relationships. It can do so by making sure that senior executives model these skills and that they clearly verbalize their expectation that such relationships will prevail in all parts and at all levels of the organization.

In addition, there must be adequate training in interpersonal skills for everyone. Assumptions to the contrary, most people are not born with, nor do they necessarily have the opportunity to learn, excellent communications skills. By devoting time and resources to the development of these competencies, the organization demonstrates the value it places on this dimension of empowerment.

Group Leadership/Membership Skills and Technical Expertise

Most of today's occupations and professions are structured around various kinds of work groups — short-term or long-standing policy committees, quality work groups, or project teams. Most groups develop ad hoc management structures that require particular, high-level competencies and a knowledge of group dynamics.

The empowering manager needs to understand the importance of both the process and the particular task in accomplishing work. He or she must know how to join a group and how to enable others to join so that their expertise and unique group skills will be recognized and valued. The ability to verbalize and participate in the establishment of group norms — especially empowerment norms that encourage each individual's active participation — is essential, as is helping define the group's reason for being in terms of successful personal and group development as well as work accomplished. An empowering manager models the skills of leadership and membership and helps others learn the concepts of functional leadership. Perhaps one of the most important skills is the ability to recognize when the time has come to disband or alter the membership; skill in this area will enable participants to move on with a sense of closure and achievement.

Of course, managers, like others, need to have technical expertise, to keep current, and to learn continually in their fields. In fact, this combination of process and knowledge competencies, when possessed by all members, leads to the success of both the group and its individual members. The members' strengths form the basis of the group's existence and define an empowering setting.

Group Productivity and Product Excellence

A successful organization is one with high levels of both group achievement and product or service quality. Empowering efforts must, therefore, focus on departmental, project, or ad hoc groups because it is in such groups that an organization's human and product or service quality come together. In an empowering organization, the association of group well-being and product quality is clearly verbalized in statements of policies and goals. Quality teams, whether they are a part of the formal organizational structure or temporary, are at the heart of empowerment.

Ability to Link Self and Group to the System

A person who is empowered sees the connections in life. He or she recognizes that no one is an island and that no action occurs in a vacuum. Each person is connected to others — in families, communities, religious denominations, political commitments, personal tastes, and so on, as well as in work. People have the freedom to choose their associations, to create their own personal systems.

The manager too creates his or her own network, recognizing the importance of relationships with peers, departments, and top management for gaining the most for his or her unit and for the system as a whole. Furthermore, an empowering manager understands how the system works, can gauge the impact of actions on it, and knows how to facilitate effective and efficient task accomplishment within it.

Interdependence, Linkages, and
Collaboration Within a System

Empowering organizations recognize and encourage the process of networking, which underlies a true systems approach to organizational structure. This process must be clearly visible to all, both in the actual structure of the organization and in its value orientation or culture. A "win-lose" attitude within a system usually bodes ill for the organization. On the other hand, organizations empower themselves when they define a "win-win" orientation through both formal and informal interactions and when a spirit of collaboration is a fundamental expectation.

Ability to Understand and Interact with the Environment

Awareness of the broader environment and attention to the interdependence of human beings and their institutions constitute another crucial managerial responsibility. It is especially important that managers recognize the implications of social and world affairs for the workplace and the task at hand. For example, inflation may affect one's co-workers and their job performance; a contract with an organization in another country may require adjustments in daily practice; or a racial issue may have an impact on certain kinds of decisions.

This dimension of empowerment may also lead a manager to be an active representative of his or her organization outside the system. Examples of such involvements are easy to find: a banker devotes every Friday afternoon to the local Chamber of Commerce; an attorney serves on the board of the local university; an assembler spends two nights a week volunteering on the crisis hotline; a university professor speaks to public groups about global society; a manager coaches a children's soccer team; and a plant supervisor helps coordinate a "meals-on-wheels" program for the neighborhood's elderly.

Awareness of External Circumstances and a
Commitment to Positively Enhancing Society

For the empowering organization this dimension is translated primarily into two sorts of actions. The first is concerned with keeping up to date with general economic factors: market fluctuations, sectoral shifts in the economy, employment statistics, and competitors' activities. On a broader scope it may include attention to Government actions such as interest rates and monetary policy as well as to worldwide corporate trends, mergers and takeovers, and foreign affairs. The more data about these factors included in the planning processes, the more likely the organization is to take full advantage of its already established strengths.

The second aspect of this organizational awareness has to do with the organization's recognition of its social and ethical responsibility. At the very least, an empowering organization designs and implements collaborative community actions and contributions. At a higher level of social responsibility, it works to empower other systems in the environment. For the organization as for the individual, an empowerment philosophy is not limited to the workplace.

CONCLUSION

Because change is the essence of any developmental process, managers and organizations must constantly fine-tune the competencies that make up the empowerment process. Once an individual or system has made the decision to become empowered and to be empowering, an ongoing process of assessment and refinement is central to the condition of parallel action empowerment. When this attitude toward change is shared by empowered and empowering managers and systems, it leads them to act in certain ways. Some of the many possible empowering interventions they may take are surveyed in Chapter 8.

CHAPTER **8**

EMPOWERING INTERVENTIONS

 Overview

Chapter 8 continues the emphasis on understanding the process of action empowerment from the point of view of both managers and organizations. It paves the way for a discussion of implementation by offering numerous suggestions of systemic, structural, programmatic, and individual/managerial action interventions — possible components of an individualized action plan. It then takes a more in-depth look at five potentially empowering interventions: Theory Z (Ouchi, 1981) applications, leadership enhancement, cross-cultural competency, training, and adhocracy.

EMPOWERING INTERVENTIONS I

The exhibits in this section present scores of possible empowering interventions. Although most are not described in detail, enough information is given to enable organizations to select the components of a customized plan for empowerment. Because there is no such thing as a standardized empowering process, planners will need to combine the interventions they choose into an action plan suitable to their own people and organization. What is empowering in one setting may not be timely or fitting in another. Moreover, the exhibit contents are in no way exhaustive; it is likely that the most creative interventions will evolve from planners' thinking about the unique qualities of their own organizations.

The interventions listed are a mixture of activities, values, attitudes, and general descriptions in four organizational and functional areas: systemic, structural, programmatic, and personal/managerial. Some suggestions fit into more than one category and, accordingly, appear several times; others, though useful elsewhere, are so fundamental to one particular category that they appear only once. Exhibits 4 through 8 offer structural, operational, and philosophical interventions drawn primarily from the conceptual foundations and pictures of empowerment described in Chapters 4, 5, and 6 and from the parallel action empowerments discussed in Chapter 7. The final category, personal/managerial interventions, is divided into two lists: (1) those related to the process of becoming empowered (Exhibit 7) and (2) those most often associated with the empowering manager (Exhibit 8). However, as pointed out in Chapter 7, a person in the process of becoming empowered may be simultaneously empowering others. Thus, the two exhibits really represent not different processes but different points on the empowerment continuum.

Acts of empowerment such as those listed are called *interventions* because they enter a "frozen" system and help it to thaw and to change form. Exhibit 9 provides the reader with a set of personal and organizational criteria for determining whether an intervention will in fact be empowering in a particular setting. It also provides a readiness check list to determine whether an organization has the necessary resources to operationalize a given plan. Most of the criteria shown must be fulfilled by each individual in the empowering loop; other conditions must be met by the organization. It is wise to apply more than one of the criteria when determining whether to implement a particular intervention or plan; the intervention that meets several criteria or preconditions is more likely to be effective in moving the system toward empowerment.

EXHIBIT 4.   Systemic Empowering Interventions

- ◆ Belief and trust in people
- ◆ Training in leadership skills
- ◆ Creation of a shared vision
- ◆ Plan for changing organizational culture

EXHIBIT 4 *(continued)*.   Systemic Empowering Interventions

- ◆ Increase in system knowledge
- ◆ Expression of equality as a value
- ◆ Orientation toward task excellence
- ◆ Clarification of organizational values
- ◆ Climate of collaboration, humanness, and enjoyment
- ◆ Atmosphere of openness, authenticity, and acceptance
- ◆ Freedom from threat
- ◆ Wide availability of information
- ◆ Expectation and encouragement of individual and organizational growth and development on the part of top management
- ◆ Climate of mutual respect, trust, and supportiveness
- ◆ Respect for physical environment
- ◆ Publication of individual and group successes
- ◆ Mutual planning norms
- ◆ Discussion of organization's expectations for the state of empowerment
- ◆ Emphasis on positive experiences with empowerment
- ◆ Valuing autonomy and managerial trust
- ◆ Clear top-management support for empowerment
- ◆ Clear ethical cornerstones
- ◆ Valuing change for growth

EXHIBIT 5.   Structural Empowering Interventions

- ◆ Flattening of the hierarchy
- ◆ Emergent organic structures
- ◆ Decentralization as appropriate
- ◆ Team and temporary group models of organization
- ◆ Open communication channels
- ◆ Bridges among all organizational levels

EXHIBIT 5 *(continued)*. Structural Empowering Interventions

◆ Smooth work-flow patterns that allow for quality, innovation, and creativity
◆ Open-access information systems
◆ Built-in assessment systems
◆ Regular use of participative structures
◆ Increased availability of and access to resources
◆ Adhocracy as a creative alternative to bureaucracy
◆ Interdependence/networking norms
◆ Commitment to respond to external circumstances and a strategy for continually scanning the environment
◆ Staffing patterns that reflect empowerment values (not traditional status differentials)

EXHIBIT 6. Programmatic Empowering Interventions

◆ Management-development activities
◆ First-line supervisory training
◆ Policies and procedures supporting empowerment values
◆ Technical education, re-education, and information programs at all levels
◆ Profit sharing
◆ Consideration of the alternative of an all-salaried work force
◆ Stress-management and wellness programs
◆ Employee-involvement programs (co-determination)
◆ Partnership orientation in labor relations and union negotiations
◆ External assessment programs
◆ Work design reflecting collaborative norms
◆ Job-enrichment experiments
◆ Creative use of sponsorships, role models, peer alliances, and mentoring
◆ Organizational orientation and socialization programs

EXHIBIT 6 (*continued*).   Programmatic Empowering Interventions

---

◆ Reward systems (promotions, special privileges, praise, money) that build "win-win" rather than "win-lose" attitudes

◆ Planned-change program (survey-research activities for all constituencies)

◆ Periodic reviews of organizational structure

◆ Individualized career-development plans (including career ladders)

◆ Benefits packages reflecting company expectations and employee needs

◆ Programs focused on life cycle of work groups: selection, orientation, training and development, working, assessment, and leaving

◆ Employee participation in writing job descriptions and standards

◆ Employee-assistance programs

◆ Modeling of empowerment behavior in all programs

EXHIBIT 7.   The Individual: Interventions for Becoming Empowered

---

◆ Willingness to become empowered

◆ Self-awareness; clarity about self; ongoing self-appraisal through review of past

◆ Improvement in listening skill

◆ Learning to recognize and verbalize group process

◆ Increased tolerance for ambiguity

◆ Sound and clear ethical base

◆ Clarification of personal values

◆ Straightforwardness

◆ Commitments made public (no hidden agendas)

◆ Willingness to join group to enhance an effort

◆ Willingness to risk new behaviors

◆ Personal openness/reduction of facades

◆ Openness to feedback (requested or not, descriptive or evaluative); cultivation of willingness to hear and be confronted

EXHIBIT 7 (*continued*).   The Individual: Interventions for Becoming Empowered

---

♦ Interpersonal competency (verbal and nonverbal), especially in the here-and-now
♦ Being invested in interactions
♦ Improved ability to resolve conflict situations
♦ Allowing, encouraging, supporting others' openness
♦ Recognition of the pain and cost of growth
♦ Involvement in personal-growth activities; sharing them with others as appropriate
♦ Progress toward becoming the person one wants to be (self-actualization)
♦ Becoming more trusting in relationships
♦ Valuing others and showing it
♦ Valuing and creating change
♦ Decreased feelings of threat, paranoia
♦ Strengthened self-esteem
♦ Heightened self-reliance
♦ Taking responsibility for self and feelings
♦ Recognition of own expertise and knowledge
♦ Seeking increased responsibility
♦ Becoming self-motivated role model
♦ Handling ambiguity and recognizing its value
♦ Patience, starting with patience with self
♦ Appreciation of new ideas and experiences
♦ Willingness to share responsibility for results of decisions
♦ Management and tolerance of high stress

EXHIBIT 8.   The Manager: Empowering Interventions

♦ Regarding empowering as a way of life
♦ Creating nonzero-sum view of power
♦ Modeling empowerment behaviors and attitudes

EXHIBIT 8 (*continued*).   The Manager: Empowering Interventions

---

◆ Timely assistance and help to others

◆ Patience, recognition that explorations take time and others have their own clocks

◆ Recognizing time required for system changes

◆ Recognizing and valuing individual differences

◆ Listening actively to others

◆ Focusing on own reactions to others

◆ Clear verbalization of issues

◆ Scrupulous confidentiality in dealing with private data

◆ Accepting mistakes of self and others and working to correct them

◆ Facilitating open communication

◆ Allowing others to take on new professional responsibilities, personal commitments

◆ Delegation of responsibility, power, work

◆ Establishment of participative-management system

◆ Extending decision making to wider group

◆ Coaching and mentoring

◆ Identification and clarification of common goals

◆ Being direct; encouraging others to be direct

◆ Improvement in interpersonal and group skills

◆ Cultivation of encouraging manner; helping to "bring people out"

◆ Openness and willingness to connect

◆ Willingness to give, receive, request feedback

◆ Enabling others to be active participants

◆ Using conflict-resolution skills (for conflicts between self and others and between or among individuals, groups, other units in the system)

◆ Acceptance of ambiguity as a step toward clarification; helping others deal with it

◆ Ability to distinguish between role and self and to humanize both

◆ Recognition of stress; development of coping skills

◆ Verbalization of support for others' selves, actions, ideas

◆ Clear statement of own values; encouraging others to act on theirs

EXHIBIT 8 (*continued*).   The Manager: Empowering Interventions

---

◆ Ensuring individuals' rights to disagree and be different

◆ Ability to praise self and others

◆ Gaining new interpersonal skills through practice

◆ Optimistic attitude about outcome of efforts

◆ Appreciation of good work

◆ Providing nonthreatening opportunities for self-assessment

◆ Willingness to re-examine self-perceptions and ways to improve

◆ Fine-tuning philosophy and behavior

◆ Ongoing assessment of progress toward empowerment of self, group, system; seeking feedback

◆ Recognition of conflict and collaboration as neutral; using them positively

◆ Clarifying expectations for all employees

◆ Establishing regular information sharing as norm

◆ Contracting for information sharing to achieve mutually beneficial results

◆ Encouragement of bridge building and networking

◆ Practicing nonjudgmental initial reactions

◆ Identifying relevant experiences for each person

◆ Inaugurating participative decision making in strategy, philosophy

◆ Improving resource availability

◆ Cultivating trustful and trustworthy atmosphere

◆ Setting own values and maintaining them, even in unfavorable environments

◆ Willingness to address issues of leadership and membership

◆ Flexible application of functional leadership

◆ Focus on process of developing an effective work group

◆ Flexibility in dealing with special needs

◆ Creation of safe environment for taking risks and assuming responsibility

◆ Ability to make use of experience as well as formal expertise; validation of own and others' experience

◆ Recognition of and respect for people's needs and feelings

EXHIBIT 8 (*continued*).   The Manager: Empowering Interventions

---

◆ Willingness to share self with others
◆ Technical/organizational/system competence
◆ Clarification of task assignment (for individuals, group, organization)
◆ Willingness to confront and explore issues, conflicts
◆ Reinforcement of others' creativity
◆ Implementation of synergistic strategies
◆ Influence over organization of work

EXHIBIT 9.   Criteria for Evaluating Empowerment Interventions

---

Personal traits	Organizational criteria
Valuing uniqueness	Recognition of
Reciprocity	interdependence
Intellectual and professional openness	Professional security
Patience	Availability of resources
Tolerance for ambiguity	Encouraging environment
Multi-dimensional thinking	Environment conducive to
Risk taking	empowerment
Confidence	Equality of opportunity
Curiosity	Freedom
Optimism	Egalitarian atmosphere
Self-confidence	Availability of time
Concentration	Common code of ethics
Self-awareness	Culture conducive to
Interpersonal skills	empowerment
Willingness to listen	Valuing of dreamers and
Spirit of cooperation	visionaries
Emotional congruity	
Enthusiasm	
Trust	
Flexibility	
Challenge	

EXHIBIT 9 (*continued*).   Criteria for Evaluating Empowerment
                                Interventions

Personal traits	Organizational criteria
Perseverance	
Stress tolerance	
Acceptance	
Valuing people	
High expectations	
Independence	
Humor	
Openness	
Commitment	
Use of imagery	
Friendliness	
Respect for others	
Personal effort	
Tolerance of difference, conflict	

Some Cautions

Literally hundreds of empowerment interventions are possible. In considering this wide universe of choice, an organization needs to keep three cautions in mind. First, the process of empowering is person centered and an individual matter: what empowers one person may not empower another. Systems initiating empowerment strategies need to be sensitive to the different impacts of activities on each individual. Moreover, each individual, in order to take an equal and active role in the process, needs to become more self-aware about what empowers him or her. Keeping track of interventions, their consequences, and how long they continue to influence the individual toward being empowered will help organizations and researchers generate further interventions.

Second, employing empowerment interventions at random will not be productive and may be harmful to organizational well-being. Empowerment usually requires major systemic changes. Quick changes in the corporate culture (e.g., quality circles) have come to be recognized as fads. They have not worked primarily because they lack the necessary foundations: commitment from top management, acceptance of structural change, a long-range time perspective, trust among people and levels, sufficient interpersonal capabilities, and appropriate reward systems. Even a well-integrated, carefully designed program that is well supported with resources and given adequate time to develop can only begin the process of creating a climate conducive to empowerment. That is not to say that the numerous interventions listed in the exhibits will not work; they may, in fact, empower an individual or a department. But if they are implemented in haphazard ways, the empowerments produced will probably remain isolated examples of short duration and insignificant impact on the system. Those implementing empowerment strategies must recognize that empowering others necessitates both philosophical and real changes and is likely to be accompanied by upheaval, discomfort, and stress. A carefully designed planning effort, however, can both reduce nonproductive effects and increase the likelihood of empowering people (see Chapter 9).

A third caution relates directly to the issue of getting started. Timely attention to it may ensure that the experience of implementing major changes of attitude and operation will be one of success rather than setback. Very few leaders, managers, or nonmanagerial employees have had direct experience with systemic empowerment. They have little idea about how to empower others, how others become empowered, how others will react, or how they themselves will react. Organizations, therefore, need to provide adequate opportunities for people to experience empowerment in safe settings where they can practice empowerment skills. Companies may also need to seek out leaders with experience in developmental programs (e.g., schools, training labs, off-site retreats). They may try to hire graduates of innovative educational programs that employ experiential-learning models, opportunities for introspection, simulations, conflict management, self-directed learning, and leadership training. Employees who have worked in other empowered settings can also facilitate an organization's progress toward becoming empowering.

EMPOWERING INTERVENTIONS II

The preceding section suggests many empowering interventions. They are not, however, part of any given empowerment method, but rather pieces to be fit together to meet unique circumstances. Another group of interventions is more holistic in orientation. Some of these interventions are broadly conceived (macro) strategies (e.g., Theory Z), and some are more detailed in scope (e.g., adhocracy). Five of these interventions — Theory Z (Ouchi, 1981), leadership enhancement, cross-cultural competency, training, and adhocracy — are presented here. Each one is closely related to the empowerment concept in theory, operation, and intention.

Theory Z (and Others)

One of the foundations of empowerment is participation. The point is not to make people *feel* that they are involved but to ensure that they really *do* influence the organization and are, therefore, empowered. Implementation of broadly based participation, according to sound principles of change, can pave the way for the implementation of other empowering strategies because participation not only empowers but also creates conditions for more innovative and far-reaching empowerment. However, *how* participation is introduced and incorporated into a system is just as important as selecting and implementing appropriate participatory models. (See Chapter 9 for more information on this process of planning a change to empowerment.)

One conceptual framework for instituting participation is called Theory Z. It was originally outlined by William Ouchi and founded on the humanistic, quality-centered, group approaches explored in the United States in the 1950s and 1960s. It has gained prominence, however, because of its success in bringing Japan to the forefront of the industrial world. In the United States Theory Z has had a rough road to acceptance and implementation. Some attribute the difficulties to differences between American and Japanese culture and values or to the contrasting needs of developed versus developing industries. Probably the major reason for its failure in the United States, however, is the lack of a well-planned implementation process.

In 1985, Charles Joiner, Jr., past president of the Mead Corporation, provided a clear, succinct description of Theory Z and defined a logical, psychologically consistent process for enacting it: "The 'Z' approach calls for organizational decisions to be made by a consensus with broad participation and a long-term view.... The important task is learning how to get all employees committed to business goals that will make a difference and how to train them at becoming the best at achieving these goals" (Joiner, 1985, p. 57). Joiner sees the basic components of Theory Z as:

◆ Long-term employment;
◆ A relatively slow process of evaluation and promotion;
◆ Broad career paths;
◆ Consensus decision making;
◆ Implicit controls, with explicit measurements;
◆ High levels of trust and egalitarianism;
◆ Holistic concern for people.

Although these elements are also in place in such successful organizations as IBM, 3M, Hewlett-Packard, and Xerox, they are not, unfortunately, common in most organizations (be they hospitals, high schools, foundries, or banks).

How then do organizations put these fundamentals of participation into operation? The following five-step process, adapted and expanded from Joiner's (1985) work, outlines the process.

Step 1. Establish leadership that has a strong belief in people and a commitment to excellence, both philosophically and operationally. Top management must be willing to entrust employees with significant responsibilities (demonstrating belief in people) and must seek continual, incremental improvement (commitment to excellence as an ongoing process).

Step 2. Build a top-management team well-grounded in teamwork skills and values. Members will combine acceptance of individual differences, trust building, and consensus decision making with strong communication skills, experience in group problem solving, and group leadership skills.

Step 3. Create a strategic vision from the bottom up in a participative manner. Once it is defined, the leadership must energetically support the vision. Next, both the vision and the process that produced it must be communicated to all members of the organization, giving them a stake in the company.

Step 4. Develop strong personnel and support systems that demonstrate congruence between management behavior and the verbalized belief in people. A necessary element of this system is a secure, long-term perspective that stabilizes the employee-employer relationship. Once this basic need is established, personnel policies such as the following need to be operationalized:

◆ Regular organization-effectiveness surveys (to maintain growth as well as to identify problems before they do any harm);

◆ A fair and competitive reward system that includes all employees in the organization's successes (i.e., profit sharing, bonuses);

◆ A selection and job-placement process that allows for self-assertion and identification with the goals and values of the Theory Z organization;

◆ A performance-review process that is consistent and growth oriented and includes surveys of management development and communications systems;

◆ Programs that encourage employee input on current issues. Responding to problems quickly reaffirms the organization's commitment to both people and quality effort.

Step 5. Build participative organization and communication structures by flattening the hierarchy, broadening the span of control, reducing staff personnel, installing systematic planning and budgeting programs, and widening each employee's area of freedom. Although the structure must operate in disciplined ways, employees must perceive it as dynamic, not restrictive. Numerous forums for participation (i.e., committees, project teams, task groups) should become the primary work units of the organization.

This five-step process of broad participation incorporates the basic principles of planned change (examined in Chapter 9). It should be clear that one does not undertake such an extensive and intensive redirection lightly. Nonetheless, Theory Z offers management some specific strategies and activities for facilitating participation within the framework of a large organization.

Enhanced Leadership

The first and second steps of Theory Z recognize the importance of leadership as an empowering intervention. Warren Bennis has made significant contributions to empowerment through his focus on leadership.

According to Bennis (1982b), leadership is an art form, a function employing both the imaginative and the analytical abilities. He sees three major tasks for today's emerging leaders: (1) envisioning the future, (2) transmitting that vision to others, and (3) empowering those others to accomplish the vision. These functions require enormous energy and an extensive menu of behavioral and conceptual options.

In the early 1980s Bennis and Nanus (1985) interviewed ninety top leaders — chief executive officers of some of the largest manufacturing organizations, university presidents, political officeholders, and coaches of winning sports teams. They found that these leaders generally share the following characteristics:

◆ A vision that inspires others;

◆ Communication skills that bring about others' support;

◆ Persistence in following through and working through setbacks;

◆ Empowerment through the design of structures that enhance others' ability to accomplish goals;

◆ Ability to respond to accomplish goals and to make adjustments in the organization based on ongoing assessment.

Of course, empowering capabilities that are appropriate for top management are not the same for leaders of smaller units within an organization. Nonetheless, the concept of functional leadership seems essential to any empowerment setting, be it a multi-national organization or a five-person project group. Leadership must be allowed to rotate to the member the group believes to be the most qualified (by experience, technical abilities, and leadership skills) to help it achieve its goals. Leadership that is empowering must include the interpersonal skills that transmit respect for and belief in others. There seems no better place for beginning to educate leadership about the importance of those skills for leadership than the work of Carl Rogers (1970) (characteristics of a helping relationship), Chris Argyris (1982) (requirements for successful development of people), and Edgar Schein (1981) (improving face-to-face relationships).

To create empowering organizations and people who are empowered, leaders at all levels must model empowering behaviors; as Likert (1967) stated, what is occurring at the very top of the organization is mirrored throughout the system. In addition to the characteristics identified by Bennis and Nanus, the empowering leader would possess the following intentions, values, and perceptual and behavioral skills (Schein, 1981, pp. 43–44):[3]

1. Self-insight and a clear sense of his or her own identity

2. Cross-cultural sensitivity: the ability to discern, and respect, other people's values

3. Cultural/moral humility: not seeing his or her own values as necessarily better than another's

4. Optimistic, proactive problem-solving orientation: the conviction that interpersonal and cross-cultural problems can be solved

5. Personal flexibility: the willingness to vary his or her response to fit the particular situation

6. Negotiation skills: the ability to explore differences creatively, to locate common ground, and to solve the problem

7. Interpersonal and cross-cultural tact: the ability to solve problems without insulting people, demeaning them, or causing them to "lose face"

8. Repair strategies and skills: the ability to resurrect, revitalize, and rebuild damaged or broken relationships

9. Patience.

Cross-Cultural Competency

One of the most important arenas for organization development is the world marketplace or the "global village." Over the past several years a greatly improved communications network and improving world relations have induced many American corporations to expand their definitions of the market. The challenge and potential of tapping not only new foreign markets but also various subcultural markets within the United States has led organizations to ask some variation of the question "How do we do it right?"

In answering this question, one might consider several lessons from history. The first comes from the late Nineteenth Century colonial period of the British Empire and presents a clear picture of failure in terms

[3]Reprinted from "Improving Face-to-Face Relationships," by E.H. Schein, SLOAN MANAGEMENT REVIEW, Winter 1981, pp. 43–52, by permission of the publisher. Copyright © 1981 by the Sloan Management Review Association. All rights reserved. This article conveys the importance of this dimension of empowerment.

of long-term consequences. People became subservient and remained so while the "reigning" British landowner or governor, who "knew best," directed, controlled, and coordinated all activity. A similar American attitude was embodied in the bullying character of *The Ugly American* (Lederer & Burdick, 1958) — the loud-mouthed, flower-shirted, cigar-smoking know-it-all who used his (or her) money to solve all problems. Remnants of this person, considerably toned down, persist in today's pin-striped business and financial people (and occasional Government liaison officers), who remain certain that they know best and will pay top dollar to get jobs done their way, regardless of the cultural milieu.

However, lessons from history can point organizations in another direction. One of these success stories is the Peace Corps. In the 1960s this agency offered American technical and organizational assistance to developing countries that wanted to develop while preserving their indigenous cultures. Both the Peace Corps and Vista (the United States organization that had a similar mission in the mountains of Appalachia and the inner cities of the Northeast and upper Midwest) had considerable success and continue to make a difference. The volunteers do not tell people what is right; they do not do it for them; and they do not impose alien cultural values.

Another cross-cultural success, more distant in time, is captured in the well-known story of the first Thanksgiving in the Plymouth Colony. This harvest feast was the culmination of a sharing of technological competencies, knowledge of the environment, and a recognition of human interdependence (with the Europeans on the receiving end).

In our own time, Philip Harris and Robert Moran (1987) have defined seven roles for managers of global enterprises: cosmopolitans, communicators, negotiators, creators of cultural collaboration, leaders in cultural change, influencers of corporate culture, and influencers of work and team cultures. These roles are strikingly similar to those of the empowering manager. Harris and Moran also outline the myriad functions that organizations active in the global marketplace must carry out: management of cross-cultural effectiveness and training, transitions, deployment, business protocol, technology transfer, and human resource development among professionals and technicians from at least two different cultures. Finally, they argue, managers must know about, and organizations must consider, not only the cultural norms, values, and customs but also the specific business conditions (structures, policies, laws) of the countries or regions with which they plan to work.

Yet another element of this cross-cultural competency is the ability to work toward genuine mutuality in assessing possibilities; defining intentions, products, and relationships; and making the decision to proceed. The benefits of such enterprises — profits, new learning, opportunities to develop — will best be achieved through two-way interactions that are strong at all levels: face-to-face relationships, intergroup communications, and corporate structures and systems.

The conditions described for these enterprises are, of course, parallel to those of empowerment. In fact, in operationalizing these cross-cultural guidelines, organizations have the opportunity to initiate (i.e., take a step or two or three toward) their own empowerment. Explorations of the philosophical and educational foundations of cross-cultural relationships can become an empowering intervention for the organization.

Training

Training is a distinct and vital dimension of today's workplace. It prepares people — human resources — to be more effective and efficient. If an organization is to develop into an empowering system, training must become a central focus of attention and effort. Training departments must be well staffed, responsive, and an integral part of all planning activities. Training cannot be relegated to second-class status and forced to subsist on budgetary leftovers.

Human-resource training relates to developing several kinds of professional knowledge and skills. The most obvious sort is technical training, such as retraining on computers, learning new applications of DNA research, practicing recent advances in welding certain alloys, or keeping current with new tax laws. Somewhat less common, but equally essential, is training in personal and professional areas such as management development, self-assessment, communications skills, supervisory training, and working with others.

In addition, organizations that want to elicit commitment and knowledgeable activity on behalf of the system must take the time to educate their members about their own ways of doing things. Organizational education may include orientation/socialization programs and training in such areas as budgeting procedures, role responsibilities, and interdepartmental planning skills. This sort of training is lacking in most organizations; the result is that many managers and employees have to spend valuable time trying to second-guess the organization.

In the last twenty years training has become a profession. Organizations have begun to realize that they depend more on their human resources than on their technological ones. (Even when new technologies are the essential element, it is vital to train people to use them.) University courses in this area as well as extensive nonacademic programs that develop professional competency are evidence of training's new professionalism.

Although training and development are not interchangeable processes, training has important developmental implications; and many of the most skilled training professionals come from the ranks of organization development practitioners. Within the organizational framework, training prepares people to take on developmental responsibilities and, thus, functions as a vital link to empowerment.

As organizations, managers, and employees commit themselves to participative planning, they must be able to appeal to training representatives for programs to accomplish given tasks. If training departments have not developed the competencies for carrying out such missions, organizations must empower them to do so.

Even beyond its developmental function and content base, good training effectively models the empowering process. On a macro level the training process begins with assessment and moves to program design, implementation, follow-up (on the job), and feedback/evaluation. The most successful training program is tailored to the system and the trainees. Like empowering managers or organizations, trainers ask, "What do you want? How can we help you get what you want? How can we follow up to see if we have helped or if we can fine-tune the learning for you?" After training they ask, "How did we do? How can we do it better? Does it fit with the organization's intentions and personal goals?"

There is also a micro dimension of training that has developed during the past twenty years and is also directly related to the concept of empowerment. This domain has to do with adult learning theory and experiential learning (described in Chapter 4). The micro framework recognizes the mature individual's ability to be an active agent in the learning process — from selecting training, to specifying expectations for outcomes, to identifying new possibilities for training content. Training today urges proactive behaviors on the part of trainees, and this action orientation — interfacing with the trainers, assisting in determining content, and helping direct the training process — harmonizes well with the empowerment concept.

As the Parallel Action Empowerment Model (see Figure 6) and the empowering interventions listed in the exhibits of this chapter indicate, many content areas provide tasks for training departments. They include personal and interpersonal skills (e.g., self-awareness, group dynamics, understanding of organizational interdependence, relationships with the external environment); management development and supervisory training; and training about empowerment itself (what, how, why, and its particular relevance for individuals and the organization). The macro and micro training processes are closely related to the sorts of personal and organizational learning necessary for empowerment and to the need for constant reassessment.

Training, in short, offers a fine tool for becoming empowered and is, in itself, empowering. It is critical, however, that the concept of empowerment not become entirely focused on training, for that could too easily lead to the assumption that empowerment is the responsibility of a specific group of people in the organization. Training has a wonderful natural relationship with empowerment, but it must be accessible to everyone. For an organization to achieve empowerment, every individual and every group must be able to empower and to be empowered.

Adhocracy

The last decade has already witnessed significant changes in how organizations regard their employees, structure work groups, and relate to their client systems. One of the most useful innovations has been the concept of *adhocracy,* the use of temporary groups brought together to accomplish particular tasks. It is a highly flexible structuring process in which the individuals most interested in and most capable of doing the work become a project team. It usually results in feelings of enhanced self-worth and achievement for group members. Table 1 presents a few of the contrasting characteristics of the old bureaucratic culture and the new culture that is emerging from adhocracy; Table 2 offers a similar contrast between the "old organization person" and the "new association person" (Harris, 1980). The clear correlation between adhocracy and empowerment suggests numerous ways in which the culture and behaviors of traditional systems are being transformed into an empowerment culture.

TABLE 1. Trends in the Movement from Disappearing Bureaucracy to Emerging Adhocracy

Disappearing bureaucracy	Emerging adhocracy
Old culture	**New culture**
System characterized by permanence, hierarchy, specialization, and division of labor	Modern systems with transient units, mobile personnel, and continual reorganization
Slow to change, usually as a result of external pressures; somewhat static in operation	Fast-moving, information-rich, dynamic organization, open to change, continually adapting
Traditionally, workers labored in sharply defined slots or roles with narrow specializations	Workers' roles flexible and temporary; project teams combine various talents and skills
Workers operated within a chain of command from top down; somewhat intractable structures and departments	Fluid, participative organizational roles, relationships, and structures; disposable divisions, work teams, ad hoc units
Primarily concerned about self-interests of organization	Primary focus on corporate social responsibility
Functioned well in stable society of routine, predictable problems and a competitive, undifferentiated environment	Functions best in a postindustrial society of cyberculture characteirzed by accelerating change and need for innovation
Vertical power concentration among a few at top levels who made all important decisions for lower echelons	Horizontal disbursement of power, responsibility; sharing of decision making with workers and consumers
Organization communication was vertical, slow, with delay normal; information available only as needed	Communications flow circular or lateral; computerized information systems open, fast; delay costly

TABLE 1 *(continued).*   Trends in the Movement from Disappearing Bureaucracy
to Emerging Adhocracy

Disappearing bureaucracy	Emerging adhocracy
Simple problem-solving mechanisms adequate for routine issues not hampered by slow-speed decision process	Complex problem solving to meet increasingly novel and unexpected problems requiring high-speed decisions
Staff/line arrangements between support and operative units	Team approach, with convergence of specializations
Required mass of moderately educated workers for routine work	Requires fewer knowledge workers and technicians
Emphasis on efficiency, profitability, plant/equipment, maintenance, capital expansion	Emphasis on people and human resource development

From "Innovating with High Achievers in HRD" by P.R. Harris, 1980, *Training and Development Journal,* 34(10), pp. 45–50. Copyright 1980, *Training and Development Journal,* American Society for Training and Development. Reprinted with permission. All rights reserved.

TABLE 2.   New Leadership Trends

Old organization man	New association person
Usually white male, who employed his energies and skills for the good of the organization, to which he was loyal	Varied competent people, including many women and minorities, employing their energies and skills for self-actualization
Considered executives and managers the "brains," while workers were the "hands"	Sees executives and managers as coordinators, consultants of mixed, temporary work teams
Looked to the corporation or agency for approval, status, economic security, reward and punishment	Mobile, self-motivated people who take economic security for granted, seek personal and

TABLE 2 *(continued).* New Leadership Trends

Old organization man	New association person
Conditioned to subservience and paid to conform; subordinated individuality, creativity for good of the organization	professional development
Joined in corporate emphasis on competition, success, and achieving quantity production	Often creative deviant who looks within self and profession for approval and fulfillment; knowledgeable worker who respects only authority of competence
Often a narrow specialist with limited education who feared change, advocated the status quo	Change agent who emphasizes cooperation, personal development, and quality product or service
By his past orientation, was ripe for future shock	Skilled in human relations and group dynamics; capable of quick, intense, temporary work relationships
Exceptional individuals were free-swinging entrepreneurs who built vast enterprises and fiercely defined rugged individualism and independence	Unafraid to enter new fields, even to pioneer the universe
	Individual who envisions and creates his or her own future; sees change as challenge; may be part of entrepreneurial group within large, complex system

Like the newer forms of training, adhocracy has both macro and micro components, both of which must be in place if it is to become a successful empowering intervention. The macro factor is structural in nature; adhocracy must be clearly visible in the design of the organization. The pools of skilled people who are able and willing to join a variety of task relationships on a temporary basis must somehow be shown on the organization chart. Initially this ad hoc strategy creates some confusion for both people and systems, and it requires enormous flexibility and fluidity to get through the early implementation period. An organization needs to facilitate the transition with a well-publicized support and education program about adhocracy, its significance to the organization and the individual, and the action plan for instituting it. The organization also must build reward systems that reinforce the new structure.

The micro aspect of adhocracy involves ensuring that excellence will result from these ad hoc relationships. For temporary task groups to be truly successful — for the individual and for the task at hand — the following group-enhancement conditions must be met:

1. Everyone who joins the group must value self and bring to the group relevant task or process skills and information.

2. Members must display interpersonal maturity, including communication skills, willingness to be proactive and take risks, and commitment to encouraging and supporting others.

3. Members must be well versed in group dynamics and leader and member roles and functions. They must be comfortable in both the content and process domains of group life.

4. Each group must define its own psychological contract. Part of that process involves attaining clarity about the task at hand, but its more significant aspect is establishing explicit group norms that describe ways of working that ensure both personal growth and job success. Using the psychological contract means verbalizing all intentions and expectations and being willing to continue the process throughout the group's life. It means not assuming, but clarifying. (The psychological contract is the most underutilized tool for helping individuals become a group and, eventually, a team.)

5. The group must demonstrate an ability to form trusting relationships. These will allow it to accept and value members, facilitate fluid information flow, identify a common vision of the goal, and design a structure to achieve that goal.

6. The group must achieve high-quality results while attending to the intelligent and economical use of resources.

7. The group must evaluate its efforts and pass along its project as-sessment. This evaluation should provide individuals with infor-mation about not only *what* they added to the group but also *how* they, as individuals, functioned within it.
8. The group members must be able to bring closure to their task relationships and move on to another opportunity to contribute, learn, and develop. The experience of closure should also enable each member to express how the group experience was useful and valuable to him or her.

These checkpoints will help determine whether people remain a collection of individuals or become a group or even — at the highest level of cohesion — a team. This development can occur only if (1) people have adequate knowledge about the task at hand; (2) they have a strong commitment to using the group to accomplish the task and achieve personal growth; and (3) they are both actualized and actual-izing.

It is clear from the foregoing that adhocracy has a dual relationship with empowerment. It provides a methodology for helping the organi-zation and its members become empowered, and it is philosophically and operationally consistent with being empowering. Adhocracy even provides a way to become better at empowering through practice, in the vein of Chris Argyris's (1982) model of double-loop learning: each time group members have a successful experience, they become more capable of being successful in their next group.

In the undergraduate management degree and the Organizational Development Leadership (ODL) certificate program at the University of West Florida, curricula are organized around teaching people how to be personally competent, how to work with others (especially in groups), and how to manage this process for the next twenty years. The following excerpt from one ODL student's paper, entitled "Empowerment and Self-Worth in Organizations," expresses his feelings about his first ex-perience in a group class:

This class has been different, and much more enjoyable. Rather than feeling competitive, I have enjoyed talking about and sharing my ideas and knowl-edge (and occasionally feelings, too) with the members of the other groups. For maybe the first time, I feel that no matter how much of myself and what

I am good at that I share with my classmates, I have not lost anything or given away an edge. In fact, by having this approach to the other groups, my classmates have shared things with me that have contributed to my growth. Through this open sharing, I have found acceptance by others of the things that are a part of me. This experience has reinforced my own feelings of self-worth, and helped encourage me to try new behaviors as I pursue personal growth.

I have noticed a parallel between these thoughts and what I wrote about at mid-term in this class. At that time, I stated that participative-management techniques did not reduce the authority of the upper-level managers who shared their power. They still maintain ultimate decision-making authority. My point was that participative-management practices help validate knowledge, skills, ideas and feelings of subordinates who are allowed to contribute of themselves to the solution and implementation of improvements in the organization. . . . When workers are empowered to contribute to the productivity of the organization, the total power of the organization is increased.

ACTION EMPOWERMENT: LOOKING BACK AND MOVING ON

This chapter's discussion of empowering interventions has defined action empowerment as a process through which managers and organizations can become empowered and empowering. It has pointed to numerous options and approaches to initiating empowerment and considered how they might be applied to various organizational and functional areas. However, although the parallel framework indicates the attitudes and values characteristic of empowering individuals and organizations, it does not provide a detailed answer to the practical question of initiating action empowerment within a large organization. Chapter 9 discusses more specific implementation issues and guidelines in an attempt to "round out" the reader's knowledge of the planning methods necessary to make empowerment a reality.

CHAPTER 9

ENACTING EMPOWERMENT

 Overview

> *Chapter 9 identifies and describes seven principles for determining whether a given activity or process is consistent with the overall process and theory of empowerment. It then provides an overview of the field of planned change, especially those dimensions relevant to enacting empowerment. The remainder of the chapter expands on the three major processes and focuses of the empowerment model: education and development of the individual self; enhancement of relationships (dyads, groups, and structures); and transformation of organizations. Of primary import in this chapter is the recognition that all individual, group, and organization development is interdependent and that this realization is particularly salient to enacting empowerment.*

As the foregoing chapters have indicated, many of the component technologies for enacting empowerment — such as the training and development fields — already exist. What are these technologies? In addition to training and management development (as emphasized in Chapter 8), the process competencies of organization development (OD) and the relatively new field of organizational transformation are fundamental components for becoming empowered and empowering. The latter offers organizations the expertise they need to institute major changes in operation, culture, or direction. A fourth technology for enacting empowerment is the study and practice of *planned change*. The one missing piece is a philosophy of empowerment to guide the process of change to an empowering system. Enacting empowerment, therefore, requires five major components:

1. An understanding of the philosophy and principles of empowerment;
2. Training and development systems;
3. An understanding of the ethics, intentions, and skills of OD;
4. A recognition of the commitment and processes of organizational transformation;
5. A solid grounding in the dynamics of planned change.

PRINCIPLES FOR ENACTING EMPOWERMENT

Although a major change in an organization can probably be accomplished using only the last four components, a genuinely radical change also requires management to understand the seven underlying principles for enacting empowerment shown in Exhibit 10.

EXHIBIT 10.   Principles of Enacting Empowerment

◆ Congruence
◆ Interdependence
◆ Excellence
◆ Integration
◆ Process and Direction . . . and Participation
◆ Coordination (Management)
◆ Investment

Principle of Congruence

The technologies used to implement empowerment must be congruent with one another as well as with the desired final state. The basic values and practices of training and development, OD, organizational transformation, and planned change harmonize well with one another and with the philosophy of empowerment. To assure congruence, therefore, organizations must provide employees with (1) the knowledge and competencies relevant to these four tools; (2) an understanding of the power of empowerment; and (3) a firm commitment to the enactment of empowerment.

Principle of Interdependence

The operating dynamic of this principle is the realization that when something happens in one arena, it will have impact on others. Although it is impossible to account for all possible ramifications of a complex situation, the principle of interdependence helps us recognize that surprises and contingencies, as well as ripples, intangibles, and planned-for outcomes, are all a part of enacting empowerment.

Principle of Excellence

This principle speaks directly to the readiness of an organization to move toward empowerment. Enacting empowerment, whether in large or small organizations, requires competence in each of the five component technologies. The role of each component must be thoroughly understood, and each component must operate at the highest level of excellence. If one of the components is not a part of the organization, it must be added. If one is not well respected, it must become so through additional commitment of resources and recognition.

Principle of Integration

Some aspects of enacting empowerment are sequential in nature; others require a nearly simultaneous integration of processes. The sequential elements relate to an organization's readiness to enact empowerment. Individual managers must attain sufficient skills before certain group and systemic processes can take hold and these group processes must be in place to give empowerment the best chance of transforming the organization. However, all of these processes must also be carefully integrated, which requires careful planning, insight into the direction of change, and ongoing assessment, of and attention to current circumstances.

Principle of Process and Direction

In enacting empowerment, perhaps the most critical factor is a shared or common vision and clarity about how to achieve it. Such a common vision combines the OD concept of the "psychological contract" and the organizational-transformation concept of attention to the transforming vision. Clearly, the greater the understanding about the goal and how it will be reached, the more likely it is to be attained. This point reminds us again of the importance of participation; no functional group or unit can be left out of the process of enacting empowerment.

A second point all too easily passed over is the need for a plan, a road map. Communicated to everyone in the organization, it gives people a frame of reference for understanding changes and for measuring progress. Again, the more people who have helped design the road map and who understand the destination and major landmarks along the way, the greater is the likelihood of success.

The final point about the direction and the plan of action is that enacting empowerment is a *process* (a means, not an end); often whole parts are altered, deleted, or redesigned as new issues arise, growth occurs at unexpected rates in different places, or a new technology or new people change the nature of the needs. Replanning is bound to be a central element of the enactment process. What is important is that the manager and the organization be moving in the same direction — toward the common vision of empowerment.

Principle of Coordination

The coordination and communication of the plan for enacting empowerment are critical. The process of enacting empowerment must belong to everyone; each person must feel the responsibility to be empowered and empowering and to understand the plan and vision of the organization. Yet research indicates that diffused leadership of complex projects usually dooms them to failure. For this reason, an empowerment manager needs to take on the task of empowering the efforts to enact empowerment in the organization.

This person must never lose track of the principles of enacting empowerment, the plan at hand, or the philosophical foundations of empowerment. He or she must serve as a role model, creating a network of communication that suffers no untimely delays or distorted messages. The network cannot become bogged down in paperwork or enmeshed in too much data nor can it be handicapped by a scarcity of information. The empowerment manager must be especially careful to keep top management, the managerial team, and the organization's employees informed and involved. Enacting empowerment can never become "Mike's baby" or "Alice's project."

Moreover, an individual's tenure in such a position and the position itself are temporary. In some organizations, the position could be relatively short lived; in others, it may be a long-term proposition. The position will cease to exist when the system decides that it has reached its empowerment goals and the empowerment processes have been stabilized. By then a system of ongoing reassessment and fine-tuning will have been established and reviewed. The empowerment manager will need to know when to stay, when to let someone else move into the role, and when to initiate closure of the processes of enacting empowerment.

Principle of Investment

In the short run most organizations will find enacting empowerment somewhat costly in terms of time, money, and people. To reach their empowerment goals, organizations must be willing to invest in new attitudes and value systems and undergo radical alteration. Such an investment is personal and cultural and means risks, responsibilities, commitment, and mistakes — at day-to-day personal levels and in the organization as a whole. Organizations must commit themselves fully to enacting empowerment and be willing to put up the resources to accomplish it. A weak investment such as "Let's give it a try for a while; what's to lose?" will fail. Empowerment cannot be a fad, nor can investing in it be imprudent. The required financial investment should be viewed carefully, and funding alternatives that dovetail with empowerment themes and behaviors should be sought. A signed blank-check approach is antithetical to empowerment, as is the failure to make adequate resources available. The realization of the interdependence of resource needs and creativity in investment of funds, time, and human resources should be a hallmark of the process of enacting empowerment.

THE PROCESS OF ENACTING EMPOWERMENT

Steps in the Process

Figure 7 presents a process model for putting these principles to work. The enacting process always begins with some awareness of empowerment on the part of an organization and its officers. Whatever the level of that awareness, it can be assessed and a baseline education strategy about empowerment instituted. Questions about whom to educate, how much, when, where, and so forth are considered at this stage. An important consideration is the level of knowledge of the chief executive officer (CEO) The first step may be to inform the CEO about empowerment and to encourage him or her to initiate the empowerment process. If the CEO has already committed the organization to empowerment as a major strategic effort, the early phase can focus on enhancing his or her foundation of knowledge.

In either case, empowerment cannot be initiated or sustained without the commitment and investment of the top managers. Recent work by consultants indicates that when top management displays an attitude of acceptance and support, organizational change is most likely to occur. Given both the complexity and personal ramifications of empowerment, such support is a precondition for implementing it on an organization-wide basis. Because what occurs at the top of an organization tends to be mirrored throughout the entire system (Likert, 1967), top management must not only learn about but also be willing to model empowerment and to be empowering.

The second major step in the enacting process is to establish the vision, which must be compelling enough to create momentum for the third step, design and implementation of a specific plan of action for change. The assessment that occurs at this stage is far more extensive than the initial assessment; it must consider the readiness of people, systems, and structure to become empowering. It will provide the data for designing a change plan that covers everything, from detailed individual and unit activities to recharting the organization and developing plans for relating to external constituencies.

The third step recognizes the need to build the change process on a continuum — from person to systems to structure. It begins by educating each person in the system about empowerment and by focusing first on management's capabilities and each member's technical competencies, then on such organizational factors as processes, systems, group relations, and structure.

Another critical part of this step is the installation of an empowerment management role — an empowerment steering committee or an individual — and a communications center to coordinate the process. The empowering manager or committee members must not, however, take on the responsibility for enacting empowerment; their role is to

FIGURE 7. Process Model for Enacting Empowerment

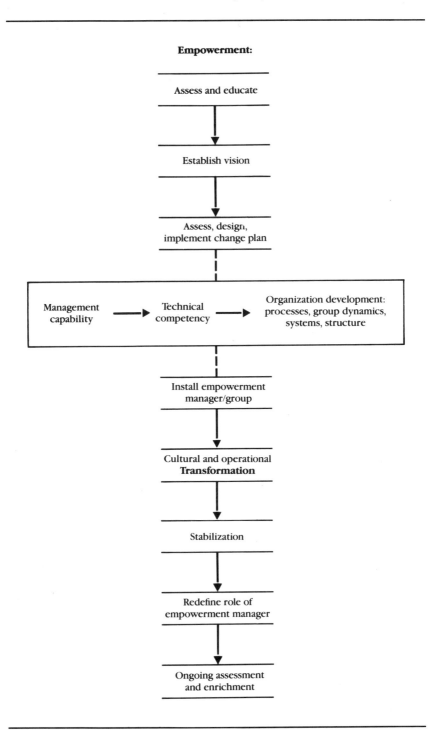

Empowerment:

Assess and educate

Establish vision

Assess, design,
implement change plan

Management
capability → Technical
competency → Organization development:
processes, group dynamics,
systems, structure

Install empowerment
manager/group

Cultural and operational
Transformation

Stabilization

Redefine role of
empowerment manager

Ongoing assessment
and enrichment

facilitate the process and, in true empowerment fashion, to model commitment to the process in accordance with the seven principles of enacting empowerment that were previously outlined. The role of empowerment management must be centered on ensuring that these principles are operationalized during the assessment, design, and implementation phases of the change plan.

Once the empowerment management and structures are in place, organizational transformation technology, especially the focus on organizational culture and operations, can be implemented. In the next stage of the process, transformation to empowerment needs to be stabilized. Those managing the process must allow adequate time for empowerment to transform the organization's culture. During this stabilization period, the empowering management role should be redefined or eliminated. Its responsibilities may be retained in a socialization program for new hires or incorporated into the assessment function.

Finally, provision must be made for ongoing assessment and for further enrichment and growth in empowering. True empowerment is a continuing process; organizations need to provide the atmosphere in which employees, departments, and systems can expand and develop their empowerment. Access to new information and perspectives from academics, other organizations, researchers, or commentators can open new doors to empowerment.

At no stage should people be pushed, cajoled, or threatened; empowerment can only be driven by the phenomenon of *readiness.* When people are ready and have an understanding of its ingredients, they will move naturally to the next phase. Moving forward before people or systems are strong and functional will weaken the foundation and make empowerment unlikely. Those managing the process of enacting empowerment must, therefore, be responsive to organizational and human readiness to proceed and be ready to facilitate empowerment — by restructuring, listening, nurturing, and informing. This is an unusual role for most designers of change, but it is thoroughly congruent with the concept of empowerment.

External Resources

Not a step in the process but highly relevant to all stages is the issue of providing internal or external guidance. Most organizations require some external help in preparing managers, learning about change processes and theory, becoming technically more competent, developing an organizational vision, understanding organizational culture, applying systems theory, setting production goals, initiating empowering financial structures, or implementing transformation.

A development trainer may provide training to everyone in the organization; or a CEO may ask the CEO and management group of another organization to appraise the operation. Evaluations may come from trainers, consultants, networking connections, customers, community members, or suppliers. The willingness to ask for and accept help from external as well as internal sources is central to enacting empowerment. A system that is open to feedback and to creative options generated outside the organization (or outside oneself) demonstrates that empowerment does not rest on a zero-sum notion of power; helping other systems to become empowered can often be empowering.

Enacting Empowerment: Processes and Focuses

As suggested before, the process of enacting empowerment needs to be visualized as a continuum — from educating with a developmental orientation, to enhancement of relationships, to transformation of organizations. It also focuses (as Figure 8 illustrates) on the three levels at

FIGURE 8. Processes and Focal Points of Enacting Empowerment

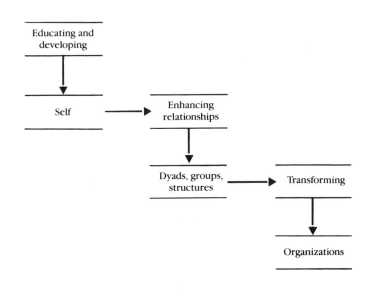

which empowerment develops: the individual self; dyads, groups, and similar structures; and organizations. Although the model indicates a one-to-one relationship between each process and level of focus (i.e., self with education, groups with enhancement, etc.), the same process of moving from education to enhancement to transformation occurs in individuals, work units, and systems as a whole.

The remainder of this chapter expands on the relations between these three processes (or stages) and the individual, group, and organizational levels at which empowerment develops. First, however, a side trip to some closely related considerations of planned change can contribute crucial insights for empowerment.

PLANNED CHANGE

In the 1960s, just as many organizations were beginning to recognize the need for major system change, a new field of knowledge about *planned change* began to gain acceptance. Although it sounds manipulative and controlling, the concept is grounded in the principle that people have both the right to determine their own futures and the capacity to do so. It assumes, with Abraham Maslow and other modern psychologists, that human beings have an innate drive toward self-development.

Practitioners of planned change define the process of change and help people and organizations identify, understand, implement, and evaluate their own changes of direction and goals. The field describes the role of the change agent as a *facilitator* and incorporates knowledge about individual change that has not previously been applied to change in systems. The most significant contributions made by theorists and practitioners of planned change include knowledge of:

◆ The process and stages of change;
◆ The principles of change;
◆ Resistance, acceptance, participation, and readiness;
◆ The change agent and his or her role and ethics.

Process and Stages

The process associated with change in individuals and organizations was clearly articulated by Kurt Lewin in 1947: in order to change, systems must first unfreeze, then change, and then refreeze into new forms. The process of unfreezing is undoubtedly the most difficult step, for both people and organizations. An understanding of the current literature about adult development and life change is fundamental to facilitating organizational change; its applicability is nicely encapsulated in the title of Gail Sheehy's book, *Passages: Predictable Crises of Adult Life* (1976).

The processes and stages of planned change are similar for most organizations; but the intentions, goals, details, and activities of each endeavor are different. An organization cannot buy a preformed plan to enact empowerment; in fact, the process of developing such a plan plays an integral role in both initiating and modeling empowerment.

Although each of the stages of the planning process has its own guidelines and special issues, the planning or design stage is particularly important. Because it gives change substance, the action plan gives people security. It must not, however, limit or restrict them. Like a road map, it should help them take advantage of new routes, incorporate scenic perspectives, or detour around roadblocks. The following is a representative list of guiding issues for designing a plan of action (adapted from Vogt et al., 1983):

1. Where and how to begin;
2. Timing and sequencing;
3. Variety and types of interventions;
4. Financial and other resource support;
5. Use of experts;
6. Innovation for assuring real success;
7. Degree and location of commitment;
8. Contingency plans and recognizing the need for them;
9. Institutionalization of change;
10. Stabilizing the system.

Three considerations provide useful beginnings for determining where to start an empowerment effort: (1) the present state of the organization; (2) certain theoretical models of empowerment, which offer reasons for starting at a particular point; and (3) others' experiences and the research on empowerment. The current state of the organization is either empowering or disempowering — as a result of organizational culture, leadership styles, reward systems, and organizational structure. An assessment of the degree to which each of these fundamental factors is empowering helps the organization identify its starting point.

Theoretical models are a second possible source of data for deciding where to begin organizational empowerment. For example, Jack Gibb's model (Greenfield, 1967) for group or system development — the trust theory — assumes the importance of widespread participation (see Chapter 4). It is based on the view that the more conscientious the efforts to affect positively the individuals in an organization, the stronger will be the basis for change in interpersonal relationships. The more the people in an organization sense themselves as secure, healthy, proactive, mature, and responsible, the more the system is enriched by their trust, commitment, and competencies (Gibb, 1964). The resulting enhanced personal and group relationships and communications can help the organization reassess its mission, define a vision, enumerate its goals and objectives more clearly, and institute structural change to accommodate those goals. Gibb's model is but one of many models that might be applied to deciding where to begin the empowering process in an organization.

The third source of data, others' experiences and research, presents a wide array of choices and information. The work of Rosabeth Kanter (1983) clearly indicates that systems should start with structural changes. Charles Joiner (1985) is convinced — with theoretical support from Rensis Likert (1967) — that the philosophy and interpersonal relationships of top management are the appropriate starting points. Warren Bennis and Burt Nanus (1985) would encourage an organization to begin with leadership development at all levels and investigators of corporate cultures would point to the need to make the components of such a culture compatible with empowerment. Edgar Schein (1985) would encourage the improvement of face-to-face relationships as fundamental to empowering people or organizations; and Albert Gore, President of Gore-Tex, might suggest beginning by clarifying the assumptions people have about working together.

Principles of Change

Of course, the most useful source of information for determining where to begin in becoming empowering is probably some combination of the three sources. When changing whole systems, however, one faces many unexpected factors. Having a set of general principles — rather than a rigid blueprint — to deal with them will help organizations maintain the empowerment focus on human beings. Exhibit 11 presents such prin-

ciples for change; their similarity to the principles for enacting empowerment indicates how fundamentally related are the theories of planned
change and empowerment.

EXHIBIT 11. Change Principles

---

1. **Principle of Interdepence**: A system has many interrelated parts;
   a change in one part affects other parts or other systems.
2. **Principle of Homeostasis**: Change upsets a system's equilibrium,
   so it may be resisted. Change must be reinforced or the system will
   revert to old patterns.
3. **Principle of Participation**: The people affected by a change
   should participate in making the change.
4. **Principle of Accurate Diagnosing**: An accurate diagnosis ensures
   a change plan aimed at the right target.
5. **Principle of Opposing Forces**: Change agents must know how to
   analyze and manage the forces operating for change as well as those
   operating against it.
6. **Principle of Proper Timing**: The time should be "ripe" for
   introducing a change.
7. **Principle of Flexibility**: Change agents and change plans need
   built-in adaptability.
8. **Principle of Inevitable Conflict**: Conflict may occur at any step
   in the planned change process.
9. **Principle of Self-understanding**: Change agents need to know
   themselves and use this knowledge in planning for change.

Adapted by permission from *Retaining Professional Nurses: A Planned Process*
(p. 244), Vogt et al., St. Louis, 1983, The C.V. Mosby Co.

Resistance, Acceptance, Participation, and Readiness

"Resistance to change is not inevitable. People may fear it as a threat to
their security and their way of doing things. On the other hand, the idea
of change can also produce pleasant anticipation of new experiences

and beliefs" (Lippitt, 1966, p. 21). Prior to the 1950s most change was forced on people. Wars, droughts, depressions, and paternalistic social systems embedded in authoritarian institutions (i.e., schools, churches, slavery) dominated people's experience. New situations, however, almost required that resistance to change be eliminated or at least reduced in impact. Early planned change researchers (Kurt Lewin, Alvin Zander, and Dorwin Cartwright) identified numerous causes of resistance to change (see Exhibit 12).

EXHIBIT 12.   Causes of Resistance to Change in Organizations

---

1. The change is not specified through documentation.
2. The purpose for the change has not been clarified or substantiated.
3. People affected by the change have not been involved in the planning for change.
4. Personal appeal has been a primary strategy used to gain acceptance for a change.
5. The operations and patterns of work groups have been disregarded.
6. Employees have not been kept informed about change.
7. Employees' worries and concerns about possible failure have not been explored or allayed.
8. Excessive work pressure is created during the implementation phase of the change.
9. Issues regarding job security and concomitant anxiety have not been attended to in open, real ways.

Adapted by permission from *Retaining Professional Nurses: A Planned Process* (p. 245), Vogt et al., St. Louis, 1983, The C.V. Mosby Co.

Once the causes were identified, the factors that prompted acceptance of change could be identified (see Exhibit 13). There is a noteworthy tendency for strategies that increase or bring about resistance to organizational change to be in conflict with the goals of empower-

EXHIBIT 13. People Will Accept an Organizational Change
If They Are. . .

1. Involved in the process of change
2. Asked to contribute (knowledge, attitudes, suggestions, feelings, opinions) to the change
3. Informed of the reasons for and advantages of the change — especially as they relate to issues of uncertainty and anxiety about the change
4. Communicated to with honesty about all facets of the change*
5. Given concrete and specific feedback about the change*
6. Respected for their feelings, whether supportive or opposed to change
7. Asked and given what assistance is needed to deal with the effects of the change on the job
8. Recognized appropriately for their specific contributions to the implementation of the change

*These two requirements tend to create an atmosphere of confidence and trust in and of themselves.

Reprinted by permission from *Retaining Professional Nurses: A Planned Process* (p. 245), Vogt et al., St. Louis, 1983, The C.V. Mosby Co.

ment; strategies that promote acceptance of change, on the other hand, tend to be congruent with the tenets of empowerment.

As these two exhibits suggest, probably the most important criterion for assuring acceptance and successful change is *participation.* It is also the most obvious point of similarity with enacting empowerment. Over the past twenty years, participation has been the principal foundation on which genuine innovation (and, in some cases, organizational survival) has rested. Moreover, the assumptions behind participation in planning (see Exhibit 14) are fundamental to empowerment in organizations.

Another factor in the acceptance or resistance to organizational change is *readiness,* which should be determined by careful data gath-

EXHIBIT 14.   Assumptions Underlying the Participative Process

---

◆ People to be affected by plans and decisions should have a part in making these plans and decisions.

◆ Such involvement leads to an investment of interest, time, and responsibility on the part of the participants.

◆ This procedure assumes the selection of realistic goals.

◆ It is a way of working toward something rather than getting away from problems.

◆ The brainstorming phases stimulate creativity through the nonjudgmental, free atmosphere.

◆ There is no preconceived way of reaching the goals.

◆ There is an emphasis on alternatives all the way through the process: alternative views, goals, and action plans.

◆ Because the work is done in group settings, there is much opportunity to build on one another's ideas and to develop collaboration.

◆ There is orderly movement from imagining, to goal selection, to diagnosing the forces in the field, to beginning initial action steps.

Adapted by permission from *Retaining Professional Nurses: A Planned Process* (p. 246), Vogt et al., St. Louis, 1983, The C.V. Mosby Co.

ering and assessment. Five criteria must be satisfied for a successful participation strategy (Vogt et al., 1983):

1. Desire to improve: people must want to become better.

2. Realization of need: people must be aware of the need for change.

3. Acceptable climate: the organization must maintain a climate conducive to the initiation and maintenance of change.

4. Need for feedback: people must know their input has been received and utilized.

5. Reward for improvements: people must believe in and experience rewards for their efforts (p. 247).

Another way to assure organizational readiness is to prepare various systems for change ahead of time. The following systems need to be ready when planning for participatory methods of change:

◆ Management systems;

◆ Technical support systems;

◆ Administrative systems;

◆ Quality systems;

◆ Communications (feedback) systems;

◆ Reward systems;

◆ Training and development systems;

◆ Bargaining systems (formal or informal).

The Change Agent and His or Her Role and Ethics

The final contribution of the planned change developers of the 1950s and 1960s is the realization that the *change agent* is central to assuring congruence between means and ends. The person's skills, values, and ethics influence process; and they must be consistent with the philosophy, intentions, and outcome of the change. The role of the empowerment manager (or committee) in enacting empowerment is similar to that of the change agent. Like the empowerment manager's, the change agent's responsibility is to be responsive and facilitative, not directive and controlling.

The role components of empowerment managers and change agents are those of any manager or key player in the enacting process. The exhibits in Chapter 8, "Empowering Interventions," outline the personal qualities and skills needed. Briefly, they must develop a deep self-awareness of their feelings about change and about their personal sense of empowerment (see Exhibit 15). Managers and facilitators must also have highly developed interpersonal skills, especially the abilities to listen, to give and receive feedback, and to cultivate an approachable personal style. They must have excellent helping skills and strong team-building abilities; bringing groups of people together to work out personal, group, and organizational issues promotes crucial learning about what it is to be empowered.

Facilitators must have a thorough conceptual understanding of both

EXHIBIT 15.   Change Agent Concerns

The following areas of concern are common to most relationships between change agent and client organization (small group, department, corporation — any system).

1. **Self-awareness**: Aware of one's own personal needs that might be served in the change agent-organization relationship

2. **Entry**: Entering (and reentering) the organization as a change agent
Able to work out a relationship that has the desired long-run consequences

3. **Diagnosis**: Examination of the motive of the organization
Problem definition and assessment of barriers

4. **Data Collection**: Agreement between organization and the change agent as to the kinds of data to be gathered and methods for doing so and with whom the data will be shared.

5. **Relationship**: Working out a constructive, mutual acceptance of each other's contribution

6. **Resource Identification and Development**: Determining those areas where the change agent and organization can be resources to the process

7. **Decision Making**: How decisions will be made and getting them accomplished and acted on

8. **Boundary Definition**: Agreements as to where the relationship and roles may proceed

9. **Ethics and Values**: Establishing and maintaining a set of values that are kept clear to the organization

10. **Plans and Alternatives**: Able to effect and successfully work out specific action plans that are tangible and accepted

11. **Change Strategy**: Change agent's capacity for change and ability to consider and devise strategies that will help the systems to carry out the change plans

12. **Terminations**: Altering the relationship as it progresses and finally terminates without undue strain to the systems involved

EXHIBIT 15 (*continued*).   Change Agent Concerns

---

13. **Evaluation**: Building in feedback mechanisms that can continually
    monitor the change experience

Adapted by permission from *Retaining Professional Nurses: A Planned Process*
(p. 277), Vogt et al., St. Louis, 1983, The C.V. Mosby Co.

planned change and empowerment. They must know about leadership
styles and skills and have significant knowledge of power and influence
(see Exhibit 16). They should be able both to use their own power
appropriately and to serve as consultants to others on *their* use of power
(influence) and its impact on empowerment efforts. These facilitators
must have highly developed skills in conflict resolution, confrontation,
and collaboration. Finally, empowerment agents must know about setting goals and designing plans to accomplish them; and they must recognize readiness as the prime initiator of movement toward goal
achievement.

EXHIBIT 16.   The Job of the Change Agent

The following aspects of the job of change agent are important in
initiating change in organization:
1. Clarification of the problem
    a. Concepts to analyze problems
    b. Skill in analysis; skill in collecting information
2. Assessing change possibilities
    a. Motivation for change
    b. Readiness to change
    c. Resistance to change
    d. Capacity to change
3. Motivations and resources of the change agent
    a. Feelings about system
    b. Technical resources to help
    c. Ability to commit time and energy

EXHIBIT 16 (*continued*).   The Job of the Change Agent

---

4. Clarification of the ethical bases for initiating change
   a. What are the goals of my change efforts?
   b. What values underlie these goals?
5. Formulating appropriate change objectives
   a. Goals emerge from a realistic diagnosis
   b. Work with inclusive group
   c. Select effective leverage points
6. Ability to take appropriate helping role
   a. Sensitive to what role is needed
   b. Ability to take it
   c. Skills in performing it
7. Building and maintaining effective relationships
   a. Neutrality — identification with goals
   b. How much dependency?
   c. When to push/when to question
8. Adapting to the phase of process
   a. Shifting from diagnosis to action planning
   b. From stimulator of ideas to stimulator of action to supporter of action
9. Acquiring/using repertoire of techniques/skills
   a. Skills in setting up learning situations
   b. Skills in providing feedback
   c. Skills in dealing with resistance

Reproduced by permission from *Retaining Professional Nurses: A Planned Process* (p. 281), Vogt et al., St. Louis, 1983, The C.V. Mosby Co.

The change agent and the empowerment manager need all of these competencies because they are role models — from whom others will learn what it means to be empowering or accepting of major change. As role models, they take on important ethical responsibilities in connection with confidentiality and nonmanipulative behavior. They need to remember that they are process consultants and facilitators — not those who determine the goals of change or carry them out. Yet they stand at a crucial point in their systems. The "ripple effect" passes on changes in one part of an organization or a person's life to all other parts of the life or system. As a result, the role of facilitator is often misunderstood. As Beer (1981) explains:

> Such a role is lonely, and it is difficult to maintain a sense of identity from which develop self-confidence and trust. Only a very confident and inter-personally competent person can play such a role. Even then, change agents require emotional and professional networks. . . . If the role is carried out effectively, it will require loosening ties with political allies, confronting people in power, and taking neutral or marginal positions with respect to important organizational matters. (p. 224)

Change and Empowerment

Throughout this section it has been evident that there is a close relationship between the concepts of planned change and empowerment, in particular their focus on methods of ensuring participation throughout the process of planning. Having a firm knowledge base in the process of planned change and the issues and principles associated with it will increase the likelihood of successful empowerment efforts.

EDUCATING AND DEVELOPING: SELF

The heart of enacting empowerment is a trilogy of education and development (of the self), enhanced relationships (between and among dyads, groups, structures), and transformations (of organizations). Earlier in the chapter the process that moves from self to others to systems was visualized as a continuum (see Figure 8). In order for the transitions from one stage to the next to occur smoothly, each step must be carefully planned and carried out in accordance with the empowerment principles shown in Exhibit 10.

The enactment process begins with each individual's capabilities and contributions, insights and concerns, understandings and readiness. It also begins with self-knowledge and the recognition that individuals, groups, organizations, and even whole societies strive for growth. The challenge of this first phase is on designing and implementing appropriate training and development programs for everyone — from the CEO to staff and line employees at all levels. In designing these programs, organizations will need to consider issues related to adult learning theory and experiential education (see Chapter 4). If the organization lacks knowledge or competence to institute such training, the first step must be to build them, for training and development are absolutely essential to empowering.

These programs must provide individuals with plentiful opportunities for self-assessment and developing heightened awareness of their particular roles in group and organizational life. The primary goal of the first stage is to develop a shared understanding of (1) the developmental perspective and (2) the concept of empowerment. These common understandings will provide linkages among all people within a system that places the highest value on human beings and their potential for growth.

First, people must become knowledgeable about human development and growth and how understanding their own and others' development can enhance the work setting. After examining their own personal development, individuals will need to consider how it affects them as members of the organization: "How am I developing as a human being? How does my development affect myself and my relations with others in the organization?" Once everyone in the system has learned about the developmental orientation, the emphasis can shift toward empowerment: the concept itself, work applications, and implications for individual selves and their work roles. The operational questions, focused this time on empowerment, are similar: "How does empowerment affect my feelings about myself and my relations with others in the organization? Am I being empowering for others?" (See Figure 9.)

In designing training modules it is often helpful to have a theoretical framework. For example, in educating people in the organization about individual development and how it is interdependent with organizational growth, we might utilize the work of Chris Argyris on human motivation (1955). Argyris identifies seven developmental movements:

1. From a state of passivity to a state of increasing self-direction.
2. From a state of dependence on others to a state of interdependence. (Argyris's term was *relative dependence*; however, his description clearly fits the current concept of *interdependence*.)
3. From being able to behave in a few ways to being able to behave in many ways.
4. From having erratic, casual, shallow, quickly dropped interests to having a deepening and widening of interests.

FIGURE 9. Empowerment and Developmental Matrix

	The concept itself	Work applications of the concept	Self-awareness (personhood)	Self-awareness (work roles)
Developmental orientation and growth				
Empowerment knowledge base				

5. From having a short time perspective to having a much broader one.
6. From being subordinate to being more equal or superordinate.
7. From a lack of self-awareness to awareness and control over one's self.

Assuming that this is the natural pattern of human development, it is evident that it is not likely to be satisfying to a normal individual to be passive, dependent, subordinate, able to do a few things, erratic, casual, and shallow in interests; to have a short time perspective; and to lack self-awareness. Nor are these characteristics likely to be empowering. Moreover, individuals with these characteristics would not be assets to an organization — especially to an organization of the 1990s and the twenty-first century. Together, they would, in fact, deter organizational growth and development as well as effectiveness and efficiency. On the other hand, individuals like those described by Argyris would contribute to an organization's growth and well-being and would be likely to attain satisfaction in life. This model of maturation thus establishes a developmental framework that individuals and organizations could utilize in promoting individual growth and enacting empowerment.

Once the issues and theories associated with human development and empowerment have been explored, an organization's trainers will need to design programs that answer specific needs that have surfaced during the initial sessions. These programs may range widely — from training in communications skills and a management-development series, to personal style inventories and sessions in giving and receiving feedback, to discussions of empowerment case studies and sharing of empowerment experiences.

The goal for this second educational effort is to ensure that the empowerment and developmental perspectives are absorbed into members' feelings and behaviors and into their thinking about actual issues and problems within the organization. Those who have major responsibility for this stage will need to model the empowerment philosophy and make sure that the training and development offered are consistent with it. They must both resist the temptation to rush this stage and recognize the appropriate time to let the organization move on to the next stage.

What capabilities should members of the organization have at the end of this phase? Even though people at various levels of the organization will have different perspectives about the fundamental issues, Exhibit 17 can serve as a starting place for considering this very complicated question. But besides specific skills, there is the question of readiness, a concept that has come up in connection with the timing of next steps. Once the goals of the training and development programs outlined above have been accomplished, a final checkpoint remains. When real applications or attempts to apply the empowerment concept to day-to-day activities begin to occur spontaneously, the personal and organizational foundations for the next step have been laid and it is time to move on.

EXHIBIT 17. Stage I. Personal Learning Foundations

◆ Knowledge about how people and systems develop and how one's own development fits within this developmental orientation
◆ Knowledge about empowerment and its implications and applications for self and the organization

EXHIBIT 17 (*continued*).   Stage I. Personal Learning Foundations

---

◆ Self-awareness
◆ Ability to take risks and a willingness to do so
◆ Interpersonal communications skills
◆ Ability to listen
◆ Knowledge about the organization's operations
◆ Knowledge of the organization's environment or context
◆ Technical competence in terms of one's job and/or role
◆ Recognition of the relationship between personal self and work
◆ Leadership/membership skills
◆ [If an executive manager, supervisor, or project coordinator] Clarity about the roles, functions, tasks, and impact of the position and the ability to develop this clarity in others
◆ Valuing of differences and disagreements (also cross-cultural sensitivity and functional skills)
◆ Ability to handle ambiguity
◆ Collaboration and competition; knowing when and where each is important
◆ Ability to network and valuing of networking
◆ Conflict and confrontation skills
◆ Trust in, appreciation of, and ability to develop self and others
◆ Opportunity to examine one's own ethics and values
◆ Proactive orientation
◆ Skills at creating meaning and purpose in ambiguous situation
◆ Ability to renew self or to seek help in doing so
◆ Helping skills/perspective, supportive and mentoring skills
◆ Ability to attend to or validate others' being
◆ Patience and perseverance to see long-term potentialities
◆ Authenticity in self and relationship with others
◆ Ability to transcend zero-sum view of power and engage in creating power in self, situations, and systems.

ENHANCED RELATIONSHIPS: DYADS, GROUPS, STRUCTURES

This second major phase of enacting empowerment focuses on developing empowering relationships within the work setting. Difficult procedural, communications, and managerial issues must be addressed at this time. Whereas the venue for the initial stage is most often nonwork environments (e.g., classrooms, off-site locations) with professional facilitators or educators, this phase shifts the focus to the "real world" — whether board room, assembly line, surgery center, or project-group meeting. The transition from separate, nonwork settings to integration with the work process will need to be well managed to encourage continued "practice" and development toward being empowered.

However, this stage represents more than a change of place. It also offers new kinds of learning concerned with working together — in face-to-face circumstances or through interdependent systems. During this time the function of "process facilitator" or empowerment manager becomes more important and more complicated. No longer are activities limited to hypothetical, relatively impersonal, and easily controllable situations. Although training is still relevant, it is but one of several empowering interventions in use. Process observations, consultation, and structural redesign are a few of the main tasks facilitated by the empowerment manager at this time. He or she may also provide testimonials, opportunities for people to share successes or frustrations, and active verbal and resource support to the process of enacting empowerment. Things start to come together at this stage, especially at individual levels. To maintain the development, practice, and application of the empowerment concept, top management will need to provide both security and some tangible rewards.

Enhancement of relationships occurs through both direct human interactions and systems communications. Improvement in human interaction develops in a sequential progression. It begins with the face-to-face skills described by Edgar Schein (presented in Chapter 4). Assuming these interpersonal foundations, plus those of the first stage, it then moves toward understanding and developing the skills needed to turn a collection of individuals into a group and, eventually, into a team. The knowledge and skill competencies that accompany this movement include, but are not limited to, those presented in Exhibit 18. The focus of such teams is not power but creating empowering relationships. The process of developing human interactions — within units, departments, or project groups and at management levels — creates readiness for moving forward in the process of enacting empowerment.

EXHIBIT 18. Knowledge and Skill Competencies of Enhanced Relationships

---

◆ Understanding group dynamics

◆ Knowing the difference between group process and group task

◆ Ability to function in the here-and-now

◆ Able to facilitate development of a work-centered psychological contract

◆ Leadership/membership skills (including functional applications)

◆ Consensus decision making

◆ Operating from a solid data base as well as personal expertise

◆ Ongoing assessment of group process and task activities

◆ Goal clarity

◆ Commitment to goals and group

◆ Esprit de corps

◆ Verbalization of feelings, conflict, and reinforcement in group settings

◆ Recognition of each person's uniqueness

◆ Willingness to collaborate with other units and valuing collaboration

---

The second area of concern for this stage is that of structural or systems interaction, which has special relevance to the organizational design of work-flow patterns and to communications systems. This is normally the place where intra-organizational competition detracts from attainment of a system's goals or decreases a group's effectiveness and efficiency. Noiseless channels of communication — those in which there is no static, only information relevant to task achievement — are most needed. Altered organizational relationships and redesigned structures to enable them to develop can empower people, groups, and the organization as a whole.

Other intra-organizational systems must also be re-examined at this stage: operations and administration systems, sociocultural systems (discussed in the last section of this chapter), client systems, and environment systems. Throughout the organization there must arise a new valuing of participation and a willingness to create super-systems that enhance a participative and interdependent relational ethic and operational framework.

Bringing about these new relationships requires expertise and investment from both internal and external sources. The capabilities and professionalism of organization development (OD) are particularly appropriate tools and can provide theoretical and practical bases for empowering relationships. Moreover, the field has an ethical and value-based orientation that is congruent with empowerment and necessary for this stage of enacting empowerment. It provides the necessary technology for helping organizations create groups of people who work together in mature, healthy, and productive ways. It has the experience to help people and organizations create unique structures and processes for accomplishing personal, group, and organizational goals. Organization development is congruent with enacting empowerment because it is a facilitative process. If a system is ready to move on to being empowered and empowering, OD provides the tools and views to facilitate the transformation.

TRANSFORMATION OF ORGANIZATIONS

The last stage of enacting empowerment is transforming organizations. Once people, information, groups, and systems are in place, the impetus to take the final hurdle has been built. Most of the structures, values, and skills to facilitate transformation to empowerment exist. Enacting empowerment still requires, however, a further step — definition and implementation of a transformational process.

A transformation to empowerment begins by reaffirming the interdependence of self, groups, processes, and organizations and the principles of empowerment. The empowerment manager (or committee) must determine how deeply the knowledge of planned change and the concept of empowerment have penetrated the organization. He or she must demonstrate members' and systems' readiness for empowerment; information-sharing systems that allow everyone to verbalize and visualize the key variables of the organization's life should be in place. Vogt and Holler (1988) describe the readiness components as:

♦ A sense of history encapsulating the organization's record of success;
♦ Vision and purpose to chart the course for the future;
♦ Beliefs and principles that establish the code of conduct;
♦ Leadership to inspire and guide the organization in conducting its affairs;
♦ Internal process for maintaining the capacity for renewal and the ability to manage change. (p. 201)

These variables point directly to the concept of *culture,* which has helped consultants, managers, CEOs, and trainers understand how to influence a system toward lasting change. A combination of norms, values, rituals, customs, history, and unspoken assumptions determine a system's culture. By this stage of the empowerment process, cultural elements have already been addressed and begun to be altered through the theory and practice of planned change, the education and development orientation, self-awareness, and relational enhancement. At this point the organization needs to affirm the changes that have occurred and decide how to sustain and increase the level of empowerment already attained by the system and its members.

One strategy is offered by Allaire and Firsirotu (1985); they recommend six steps, which are paraphrased and listed below.

Step 1. Making a diagnosis. Asking "What is the relation between the firm's culture and structure and its external environment? Is it ready to adjust to future changes?"

Step 2. Formulating a "meta-strategy" for radical change. Identifying and implementing new strategies, structures, systems, and supporting values to support major system change.

Step 3. Assessing the organization's present culture and structure. Looking at such cultural variables as assumptions, expectations, values, frames of reference, stories, legends, myths, history, valued behavior, socialization processes, leadership, cultural reinforcement, and employee involvement.

Step 4. Defining the organization's cultural and structural goals. Describing the new system (culture and structure) in terms of the variables listed in Step 3.

Step 5. Proposing a broad agenda for radical change. Recognizing that radical change means changing the culture and the mindsets of individuals. This step includes such broadly based change activities as political and symbolic actions and empowering change agents to deal with micro and process issues.

Step 6. Stabilizing the organization. Attending to consistency in the domains of personal behavior, culture, and organizational structure.

In several respects Allaire and Firsirotu's model is similar to the process of empowerment described in this book; most change technology is constant in terms of processes and stages, and changes in organizational culture are at the heart of any transformation. There are, however, important differences between the two models. First, their model does not necessarily lead to a higher level of operation and personal existence, nor to ongoing assessment and further enhancement. Moreover, their model places responsibility for radical change squarely on the shoulders of the organization's leaders, although it recognizes that participation is necessary. As stated earlier, transformation to empowerment requires top-management commitment, investment, and leadership; but an empowered and empowering organization can only be built on a solid foundation of developing people and interdependent systems.

Another of the methods that systems have used to initiate cultural transformation is the "vision retreat" (or seminar), which helps people visualize the future and explore how it can be reached. The process of envisioning change, of course, needs to occur at all levels of the organization; top management's role, in addition to contributing its own vision, is to integrate the various visions into one that captures the essence of empowerment. As emphasized earlier, the process is as important to empowerment as the shape of the final "product." This is especially true at the final stage; by then, members have become far more capable of working together and of understanding the personal and relational issues of doing so. The vision will solidify the new cultural dynamics and help reshape the organizational culture. It is, in fact, the first foundation of organizational transformation (as shown in Exhibit 19).

EXHIBIT 19. Foundations of Organizational Transformation

◆ Create a vision
◆ Prepare the culture
◆ Ensure belonging
◆ Implement participation
◆ Understand the nature of work

One other conceptualization is relevant to the final stage of enacting empowerment. In *The Change Masters* (Kanter, 1983) the author describes five building blocks that "increase the company's capacity to meet new challenges." Like so many others, Kanter has incorporated a developmental perspective by emphasizing the cumulative effect of change variables. Her building blocks are:

1. Departures from tradition: Keeping in mind that it is essential to confront tradition.

2. Crisis or galvanizing event: Recognizing that enactment is a galvanizing event; as it progresses, it precipitates further action to avoid crisis.

3. Strategic decisions: Identifying important events in the change process and key sources of change strategy. Adhering to a set plan will probably not result in the desired outcome.

4. Individual prime movers: Identifying change agents throughout the organizational system. Success in a change is dependent not only on the support of the CEO and top management but also on the input and commitment of others who are involved and who play a significant role in determining whether the change is accepted.

5. Action vehicles: Building momentum for change through the vehicles of a shared road map, training, teamwork, new systems, and the empowerment-management function. (This force includes all the

variables previously described for building momentum to move to action empowerment.)

Transformation means new ways of being. This final stage of enacting empowerment provides for these new ways of becoming and being. Although transforming organizations is extremely difficult, within the context of the framework of enacting empowerment it can be a natural process that brings people and their institutions together in ways that remind them of their wholeness and the connections among them.

A REVIEW AND FUTURE CONSIDERATIONS

This chapter has presented a detailed look at the process and stages of creating an empowering organization. It has emphasized that the model rests on a solid foundation of training and development, participation, knowledge, interpersonal capability, leadership, and culture. Perhaps most fundamentally, the recommendations recognize Marsenich's (1983) four "steps of change" as the avenue to organizational metamorphosis: awareness, understanding, acceptance, and change. The authors hope the discussion has opened doors for readers and given them and their organizations guidance for becoming empowered and for being empowering.

Chapter 10 brings the description of empowerment to closure and envisions what it can achieve in the future. Perhaps the organizations pictured there, along with the pockets of empowerment that already exist, are the organizations of the future.

EMPOWERMENT TODAY AND TOMORROW: A PARADIGM OF CHOICE

 Overview

The closing chapter looks briefly at the future work life of empowered and empowering employees and managers. It then describes how empowerment might look in the future in five settings: education, health care, law, government, and business. It also presents nine trends for the 1990s and considers what they could contribute to an empowering future. The chapter concludes with a reminder that organizations have a choice between power that creates power—through enabling, educating, informing, including, and developing—or power that limits the growth of people and structures.

Are the models of future organizations based more on the experiences of the past or on visions of the future? Can organizations create models and ideals that go beyond their historical roots? The effort to transcend past histories of organizational abuse and alienation is a significant challenge. As the next century approaches there is an opportunity to design and develop new organizations that are as different from today's as today's are from the medieval manors, slave plantations, and sweat shops of past centuries.

In this century considerable progress has been made, and the growth curve need not flatten out. The potential for further improvement exists if a vision of progress is created. The empowerment per-spective offers such a vision. The process of liberation and the practice of democracy are ideals not fully realized in American society; they re-main destinations toward which the nation is journeying. American or-ganizations too must choose between striving to achieve the democratic principles of the Constitution in their work environments or allowing complacency to lull them into accepting yesterday's legacies as tomor-row's vision. Failing to work toward fulfillment of the democratic vision will not only result in personal and social disappointment; it will greatly reduce America's competitiveness in a global marketplace. In its short history, the American success story has been based on the dynamic and forward-looking nature of its society. If this dynamism is to propel our organizations forward it must come from a democratic orientation that balances power and responsibility in more hands.

What these new organizational forms might look like is the subject of the following discussion. While no single vision can direct such a vital and diverse country as the United States, a shared goal of increasing power through empowerment can generate the energy needed for such a renewal.

WHAT COULD BE: AN INDIVIDUAL'S DAILY WORK LIFE

In many respects the daily life of an empowered member of a future organization might resemble the present-day experiences of profession-als. The difference might well be that a far greater number of individuals will share professional perquisites and responsibilities for the organiza-tion's success. Most members of the future work force will be salaried and work under contracts that specify the expectations and responsibil-ities associated with their jobs.

From the hiring process to the phased-in retirement program, the employee of the future will be more carefully selected, socialized, and helped to make transitions. Individuals will be selected for their tech-nical and interpersonal skills. Because the organizations of the future will rely heavily on collaborative efforts, the role of supervisor or over-seer will no longer exist; people who need close supervision will find it difficult to be hired.

In the future the central Government, along with state and com-munity agencies, will probably determine that high-quality educational experiences are essential for every citizen and will move to provide them. Although such provision is reflective of the democratic ideal of an educated citizenry, it will also be a response to a competitive global economy. Without it, the United States could slip to the status of a second-rate economic power.

Within organizations, workers will be assisted in achieving the educational growth in technical and interpersonal skills needed for personal and organizational success. Each day they will receive information briefings through live interactions and videotape libraries. They will have access, at the nearest computer terminal, to current information about the organization and its environment.

As part of work teams and temporary task forces, the average worker will experience many different leadership styles. People who are technically and interpersonally very capable will be sought out as leaders. The sharing of leadership responsibilities will be a normal part of the organization's operating style, and an ethic of helping one another develop leadership qualities will prevail. An informal tradition of more experienced and skilled people assisting others will be integral to the organization's culture. The benefits of mentoring and supporting others' development will be formally recognized in the reward system. Decisions about leadership responsibilities will be discussed, and contracts and agreements will set out clear task and process goals.

Structurally, future organizations will be flexible enough to change to meet new demands from the environment. The structure will empower people by lowering barriers to asking or seeking help from anyone — and anywhere — in the organization. Status differentials will be very much reduced in this flattened hierarchy; the knowledge of who is responsible for what will be as accessible as the nearest computer terminal. Information will move more quickly, and there will be a minimum of secrecy and confidential information.

Finally, members of the future organization will be more self-actualized, more certain of who they are and what they are doing. They will take distinct pride in their accomplishments and experience the organization as a supportive human community. Home, community, and spiritual life will be important to the actualizing worker. These individuals of the future will not be models of perfection, but they will be empowered — by basic education, skills and knowledge training, good leadership and mentoring, availability of resources, job and organizational structure, and a culture that helps them move toward self-actualization.

WHAT COMPETENCIES ARE NEEDED:
THE MANAGER'S EMPOWERMENT ROLE

The empowered organization will depend on managers who create empowerment within the various working environments. To be effective in doing so they will have a firm belief in the empowerment paradigm: power can and should be created and can be a positive factor in reaching individual and organizational goals. Managers will have the opportunity to grow into the central role characteristics introduced in Chapter 3 — informing, motivating, planning, evaluating, decision making, and developing.

Each day the manager of the future will take time to review what is occurring and ask himself or herself what additional information or resources people might need. The roles of information facilitator and educator, which every manager of the future will need to take on, will be critical to the organization's effectiveness. The organization of the future will depend on these expanded roles for managers; it will demand highly developed technical skills and expertise in information sharing and in the sophisticated interpersonal skills needed to empower others.

The manager of the future will also be responsible for the day-to-day motivational climate of the organization in two categories. First, he or she will need to ensure safe, healthy, and fairly compensated conditions of employment. Second, and more important, the manager of the future will assist and support the work team; like a good coach, he or she will make sure the team is playing on a level field with fair rules and the right equipment. An empowered work team produces its own motivation; the manager's job will be to help build the team and see that sustained high performance does not produce so much stress that the chances for achieving long-term success are ruined.

Another daily activity of the manager will be seeing that the strategic plans established in a collaborative and participative process are being addressed at a tactical level. He or she will serve as a facilitator, helping to coordinate the work flow of the responsible individuals and teams. The success of specialists will depend very heavily on the manager's integrative skills. Although many of the traditional managerial responsibilities will be maintained, they will be carried out in a far more collaborative fashion than is now the case.

The manager of the future will also fill the role of evaluator and counselor to help individuals evaluate themselves. He or she will assess the unit, division, or organization as a whole, seeking out excellence to praise, noticing previously unnoticed good deeds, and offering appreciation to those who are working hard for the common cause.

In decision making too the manager will play a facilitative role, ensuring that decisions are made as close as possible to the point where they will be carried out. Getting the decision and the action together and helping design a decision-making process that fits the organization's demands and responds to its environment will be one of the major challenges of the future manager. The empowering manager will also provide expertise and advice about the best place (and people) to make particular decisions. And, of course, he or she will have the responsibility to communicate the decision clearly to those who will carry it out and to others who need to know.

Finally, every day the manager will need to take a quiet moment to reflect on how well he or she helped develop the individual's, group's, and organization's abilities to work effectively. The need to support and encourage the growth capacity of individuals and the organization will be the fundamental assumption underlying all of the manager's actions.

This developer role will be celebrated and never taken for granted in the organization of the future. Special events and congratulations will encourage managers and all members of the organization to maintain a developmental perspective. At least twice a year the developmental goals of individuals and the organization as a whole will be reviewed, evaluated, and either affirmed or redesigned.

As organization development becomes more and more important to survival in an increasingly competitive world, the empowerment perspective will take on more importance. Starting with self-empowerment, the manager of the future will play an essential role in creating the energy needed for the organization's social and economic gains.

WHAT CAN BE: FIVE SETTINGS FOR FUTURE EMPOWERMENT

There are three basic approaches to evaluating the performance of an organization. The most common, short-term, and overly simplistic evaluative model is that of financial health — either profitability or operation within a set budget. Financial health is a useful measure of short-term success if kept in perspective.

The mid-term measures, of the quality of the goods and services produced, are more complicated. It is not as easy to manage quality as it is to manage the financial reality, for quality must be intrinsic to every part of an organization and is not as easy to control as a balance statement or a budget record. Quality outputs demand quality inputs from individuals and groups empowered to use their skills and abilities to do the best possible job. When cost-saving goals override quality goals, short-term results may not reflect the trade-offs, but the mid- to long-term story may be very different. Most organizations, therefore, need a longer-than-quarterly time horizon for evaluating success.

The long-term measure of an organization's success is the appropriate one for empowered organizations. It is, like the primary goal of the empowering manager, development: being better this year than last and being committed to being even better next year. This development concept can be separated into two measures of health: (1) the organization's ability to improve its production of goods and services (using both effectiveness and efficiency as criteria) and (2) the human growth and development (empowerment) that occurs within the organization.

The following descriptions of five empowered fields of the future — education, health care, law, government, and business — suggest that there are now organizations in each of these fields capable of empowering themselves. The discussion highlights how these organizations might create empowerment scenarios to assist them in meeting their short-, medium-, and long-term goals of success.

Education

As suggested in Chapter 4, the fundamental goal of all educators is empowerment: helping people become capable of setting and reaching goals for individual and social ends. But, according to classical assumptions, educating others requires first educating the teacher. A major reform of our educational institutions under these conditions would require an impractically long period of re-education. Moreover, on an individual basis, this strategy can work only if the world stays stable long enough to allow teachers to pass on their knowledge before it becomes obsolete. The organizational solution, of course, is to use the process of empowerment to engage people in a mutual discovery of how and what to teach today to prepare people for tomorrow.

Empowered educational organizations of the future will ask these questions on a regular basis, for in a dynamic world the answer cannot be given once and for always. These organizations will have to open themselves to more members of their own communities and seek information from them about what they should be teaching and how. School and community partnerships will reflect the "stakeholder" concept of shared responsibility and the understanding that collaboration produces synergistic rewards for all concerned. Parents, businesses, volunteer groups, local government, and students will help teachers and administrators decide what and how to teach. Some version of the empowerment process described in this book will be a core component of educational renewal.

The educational organizations of the future will *model* learning, not try to force it on an unreceptive audience. When students do not feel empowered in their learning, only pressures for conformity — ultimately futile — will motivate them to learn. In future empowering learning situations, the line of demarcation between teacher and student will blur; the process of learning together will create an even deeper base of knowledge. Learning skills, as well as fundamental content, will be emphasized. By opening themselves to the community, schools will demonstrate that basic skills and the ability to learn are crucial to a work life characterized by unexpected demands.

Empowered educational organizations will also provide needed support services to their communities. Teacher-mentors will have time to be close to several students; and, as leaders, they will help develop other leaders. Shared responsibility for learning will be a priority, and the dependency pattern will be broken as learners move into organizations expecting to be responsible and empowered.

If the country cares about its long-term future, the resources to make quality education a primary goal and a rewarding occupation will become available. If they are not, public education will become a dumping ground and private educational organizations will carry the heavy burden of educating an empowered work force. In that situation, the trend toward a two-tier society will result in ever-more-severe social problems; and a lack of qualified and empowered workers will impede organizations' efforts to compete internationally. If it gets to the point where Americans start purchasing education from foreign competitors, rather than having people come to this country for education, the country will have lost one of its strongest comparative advantages — an enlightened and well-educated work force.

If, on the other hand, the educational organizations of the future model the empowerment potential, they will remain competitive. By committing themselves to achieving success in terms of short-, mid-, and long-term measures, they will become the nurturing grounds of self-actualization and empowerment.

Health Care

Like the educational organization, the health-care organization delivers essential services to the community and requires a cooperative relationship with its clients. It needs an empowered patient, one who not only can assist in the diagnostic stage but also can work with health professionals in maintaining good health. As the emphasis of health care shifts toward prevention of illness and promotion of health, the organization's mission will change. As the boundaries between it and its community dissolve, people will come to the organization to learn how to improve and maintain their health, not just to get well.

These changes in mission and perspective will call for major changes in the way health-care organizations operate. Demands will be increased for teams of medical experts, teachers, and care givers to work with many more people. In order to do this, teams will move out into the community to listen, educate, inform, and empower. To perform these new roles they will need to educate and empower themselves.

If major changes do not occur in this field soon, however, the long-term viability of the health-care institutions will be threatened. The external pressures demanding that a growing percentage of national income be devoted to health care have already produced a crisis in costs: the costs of repairing damaged health have reached levels the country seems unwilling to pay. Even a preventive-care system, which should ultimately lower medical costs, will probably require some form of Government intervention.

Health-care organizations will only be able to change quickly enough to meet this crisis and lead in developing new systems if they become empowered environments. Institutions with bureaucratic cultures that are resistant to change will become less and less important.

Although the rigidities and status differentials in place in many health-care settings will slow down response time, empowering leadership will be working to educate and support those most resistant to changes.

Law

Of the organizations facing a changing environment, the legal profession has exerted itself the most actively to influence its environment. In fact, its success in doing so has created public disenchantment and a tarnished image of the practice of law. In this change, however, are the seeds of its own rebirth as an honored profession. The legal profession, a mediative and negotiating mechanism in human relationships, presents an opportunity for empowerment.

In the future, the empowerment phenomenon will be greatly aided by the availability of legal counsel for all citizens. Both in their traditional adversarial roles and in their increasingly important negotiating role, attorneys will speed social change and increase the rights and legal protection of more people. As the saturation point is reached in the supply of trial lawyers and as caps are placed on financial settlements in damage suits, attorneys, law firms, and bar associations will re-evaluate the profession.

Far-sighted attorneys and firms will be active in cases of empowering individuals in conflict with organizations over issues of liability associated with stress and alienation in the work place. Lawyers will represent not only people bringing damage suits but also those seeking to institute changes to *prevent* damages.

In a world where more and more organizations will be attempting to empower their employees, the emergence of heretofore hidden conflicts will create opportunities for new kinds of legal interventions. Legal organizations will, increasingly, develop their capacities to assist in finding win-win solutions rather than engaging in adversarial win-lose tactics. As lawyers work together to resolve disputes and help people prevent conflict by forming more effective preventive systems and contracting processes, the public image of the profession will improve.

Government

In a democratic society, though public organizations are often not as vulnerable to change in the short or middle term, there is tremendous potential for dramatic change in the long run. The important social changes now affecting every other field will eventually catch up with the public sector.

A typical large bureaucracy creates a powerful and generally safe environment for itself. Since the presidency of Franklin Delano Roosevelt, Federal agencies have grown in size and power; more recently, however, there has been declining public support for these protected enclaves. The strategy of the future agency will need to be more proactive, identifying public needs not being met and moving to meet them. An empowered organization will be more able to do this than an inflexible bureaucracy; these future public organizations will stake out territories in which they can provide services and secure their own futures.

Empowered government organizations at all levels will also work more closely with citizen groups and legislative bodies to educate, inform, and empower in ways that reflect the principles of an open democratic society.

Many of the legal protections to empower civil servants presently exist in civil service law; the demands on them for responsibility, however, are not as firmly in place. As public demands of fiscal accountability strengthen, job performance will become an important measure. The question posed of an empowered agency will not be "How well did you conform to the rules?" but "How effectively did you get your job done within the rules?" When job-performance values come to the fore, the public will see results that many have caused to expect from the public sector.

The use of agency task forces and special teams to carry out specific projects will increase to meet heightened governmental responsibilities. Outsiders will come and go in government on an as-needed basis, and the career civil servant will take on more responsibility for facilitating the effective use of these human resources. Pride in government service will return, and there will be respect for the empowered organizations that look for ways to serve their constituencies. Moreover, government service will demand higher levels of professional responsibility as the country comes under increasing economic pressure from abroad. Government agencies and departments will meet these pressures by restructuring themselves to empower their service providers.

Business

As the organization most likely to respond to change, the business firm operating in an increasingly competitive world market will develop the means for increasing its power. As pressures for quality goods and services grow, business organizations will need to get the most from all their members and managers. These empowered organizations will be healthy but demanding places to work, places in which individual and organizational power and responsibility will be increased through development. An empowered, decentralized, more autonomous work force will place more and more responsibility on the individual.

Organizations of the future will maintain an appreciation of what they have accomplished, as well as a continued commitment to the long-term goal of progress and renewal. Managers and leaders will support and encourage even better performance, taking on new responsibilities for providing resources and facilitating information flow. They will also recognize the need to integrate all functions of the business with a strategic plan and conduct ongoing evaluations of each unit's contribution to that plan.

These organizations will look very different in form and structure from present-day models. The information/service economy and the global village concept will support the emergence of small specialized teams or task forces capable of rapid development anywhere in the world. Organizations will evolve toward loosely organized networks; temporary associations of individuals, groups, and even organizations will become the norm. Speed of response and sophisticated technology will be the hallmarks of success for these worldwide organizations.

Business will demonstrate the progress of human evolution toward an empowerment perspective. Instead of control and coercion, the bywords will be collaboration, coalition, coordination, and cooperation. At all levels leaders will inspire and direct and, in their turn, be inspired and directed by others in situations requiring different leadership abilities. Although global economic competition will be a key driving force behind these new arrangements, visions of human progress will inspire and motivate individuals to achieve results demonstrating their belief that human progress is indeed possible.

NINE TRENDS FOR THE 1990S

The trends shaping the remaining years of this century will produce the empowering organizations of the future. Like the developing human being, an organization is affected by its culture. The following interconnected cultural trends will continue to influence the social and organizational culture of the twenty-first century:

♦ Global competition and integration;

♦ Decentralization and entrepreneurship;

♦ The relationship between participatory and democratic skills;

♦ Ambiguity/conflict;

♦ Organization development $\longrightarrow$ transformation;

♦ Recreated community;

♦ Spiritual awakening;

♦ Renewed family systems;

♦ Exponential emergence of empowerment.

These trends reflect most clearly the major pressures that managers and their organizations are increasingly feeling. The challenge is to use them to drive the empowerment process and to increase individual and organizational capacities for growth.

Global Competition and Integration

In the four decades since World War II, the international economic reality has changed significantly. Global competition, not the supremacy of one or two national powers, is the norm. Of all the trends discussed, this one is the least likely to change. The world has been on this path since the days of Marco Polo and the speed of change continues to increase. Organizations that do not integrate themselves into this new world economy are not likely to survive.

In the United States the one window of opportunity for an organization to increase its competitive edge is to become a more powerful (i.e., high-performing) system. This can occur only if individuals within the organization develop the blend of responsibility and autonomy implicit in the empowerment philosophy.

Decentralization and the Entrepreneurial Age

The 1980s have seen the emergence of an age of small-business ventures. This trend is partly in response to the global situation but is also reflective of a favorable economic environment and the American spirit of capitalism. The advantage of the small, newly formed business is that it can shape itself to meet current challenges, instead of relying on past traditions and inflated hierarchies. This development has also given the decentralization strategy greater credibility. Although many older, heavily bureaucratized American industries (e.g., steel) have reacted to the new climate sluggishly, some large firms have responded by decentralizing, flattening their hierarchies, and creating stand-alone profit centers.

The recent economic record suggests that the power scattered among twenty small, well-run organizations can overpower one over-structured hierarchy of twenty levels. This trend is an especially powerful force for empowerment when each of the twenty small firms is employee owned.

The Relationship Between Participatory and Democratic Skills

The new age of entrepreneurship demands that people develop the democratic skills necessary to function effectively in empowered settings. In the past, similar calls for a participatory management style were seldom accompanied by adequate training and opportunities for workers to develop these skills. Managers were left in the precarious position of trying to introduce elements of democratic organization into environments where few had any experience with — or commitment to — responsible participation.

A similar trend toward democratic structures can be seen in educational models that provide people an early opportunity to develop participatory skills. Moreover, there is an increasing number of voluntary organizations (e.g., social-advocacy associations and some feminist groups) in which leadership is shared. Managers and other organization leaders need to demand that training centers offer programs in these skills. The creation of new empowering organizations is directly linked to their development. Although the emergence of these skills represents a significant trend, there are countervailing influences that restrain the effort to empower people to function effectively in democratic organizations.

Ambiguity/Conflict

To operate effectively in a period of rapid and continual change, people must be able to deal with situations and uncertainties that create conflict. The problems of alcohol and drug abuse mirror a similar need to develop skills to deal effectively and democratically in settings characterized by conflict and ambiguity. Since there is virtually no possibility that change can be avoided, some schools, business organizations, and health-care agencies are now training facilitators to help people deal with conflict and ambiguity. Legal, religious, and community groups are also helping develop these proactive skills.

Organization Development ⟶ Transformation

The increased influence of the organization development (OD) outlook is one of the most encouraging trends. This development must go hand in hand with empowerment to have a long-term chance of success. Since it emerged in the 1960s, this field of applied behavioral science has spread to organizations everywhere. Using a developmental perspective and a strategy of participation and education, OD has helped numerous American organizations become more humanistic, responsive, and productive — in short, empowered. Recently OD has moved onto new conceptual ground to examine how the transformation process can occur more rapidly. As the twenty-first century approaches, there is more and more evidence that organizations and individuals can manage their own destinies and become competitive in the global market.

Community Recreated

Like the organizations that are finding within themselves the resources to redesign their structures and relationships, communities are searching for new ways of living together and developing safer and more supportive environments. Community building is occurring in unique ways to which the geographic and relational limits of the past are no longer relevant. A sense of community is now being reflected in loose networks, new religious organizations, self-help groups, neighborhood-watch associations, and all kinds of new social groupings. People are creating new connections everywhere. As the human need for community becomes more visible, it becomes even clearer that the collaborative spirit of empowerment is fundamental to human life.

Spiritual Awakening

Although this is not the Age of Aquarius, in these waning years of the century there is a growing emphasis on spiritual values and searches. People are seeking something to transcend their everyday existences; they are asking for more out of life and, frequently, desiring to give more.

The drive to empower an organization is reflective of that spiritual search for meaning and purpose in these turbulent times.

The spiritual search can also be an active element of an empowerment process that demands more of self. Complacency, apathy, and cynicism are not adjuncts of spiritual enlightenment, nor are they helpful to the creation of empowered organizations. The search for a vision of what can be is common to the empowerment and spiritual paths. The strength of this trend indicates that such paths have increasing appeal.

Renewed Family Systems

One of the greatest challenges facing the empowered organization is the effort to establish a healthy balance of home- and work-life commitments. If empowerment translates into a sacrifice of family, its long-term results will be negative. In the past, this has occurred when the energy and commitment created by a small empowered group within the organization has induced its members to take on a disproportionate share of responsibilities. The resultant degradation of the family systems and the eventual burnout of the overworked individuals is a poignant cautionary tale. The long-term capacity for empowerment must develop within a healthy balance of home and work life.

Recently rapid changes in family systems make it difficult to predict an outcome; perhaps new systems will develop in step with more empowered organizations. Even now, however, it is possible to recognize that the composition and structure of the new family will be shaped by the high value placed on both the grounding of "home" and the opportunity to contribute and achieve in other settings.

Empowerment Emerges Exponentially

As the preceding eight trends continue into the future, they will feed off the overall trend of empowerment. Increasing the individual's power and responsibilities is a naturally synergistic process that grows exponentially. The direction of change is not always easy to recognize in the short term; but looking back to the normal conditions of organizational life in the 1950s and 1960s makes it very obvious. When Chris Argyris wrote *Personality and Organization* (1957) and when William H. Whyte published *The Organization Man* (1956), there was an implicit acceptance of hierarchical relationships and organizations that were slow to change. Since then, the pace of change has quickened. World events, social changes, and the notion of organizational transformation through empowerment have produced new models of what organizational life can be like. They have also brought new, and sometimes difficult, choices for the organization. Perhaps the most important development of this period has been the reconceptualization of power.

CONCLUSION: THE NATURE OF THE JOURNEY

Action Empowerment Revisited

Figure 10 illustrates the dynamic flow of events in which power drives the actions of an organization, either toward an empowering process of creating power or a controlling process of limiting power. The result is either a positive power flow or a self-defeating power drain.

The model starts with an assumption that the core ingredient in all organizational life is power and that organizations are involved in the collective creation of this basic human energy. Without it, nothing happens. A channeling of energy occurs as a motivational thrust; that is, motivation is energy moving in a particular direction or focus of power. Decisions and actions represented by specific behaviors are the results of each individual's motivation. These behaviors are then managed, or influenced, to create the planning, leading, organizing, and developing actions that sharpen the focus on the purposes of the organization.

Another set of process or on-line influence factors affect what the organization is to become. These process factors are a constantly applied set of skills and needs that help produce the organization's adaptation response. This reaction response results in consequences that can be seen in two ways: (1) negative consequences that drain power in a self-defeating cycle; and (2) the positive consequences, the way power is experienced when managed from an empowering perspective, which produces more power. The positive outcomes also reinforce the action potential — the organization's ability to respond to its environment and to take action that is supportive of its own development and capacity to accomplish its goals. The entire process occurs within an environmental context of cultural, social, and organizational norms.

If an organization is stuck on a negative-consequence path and is using up its power potential, the mechanism for changing that self-defeating process begins with an awareness of how power is managed in the organization. If it is managed out of existence by a rigidly

FIGURE 10. The Power Base of Action Empowerment

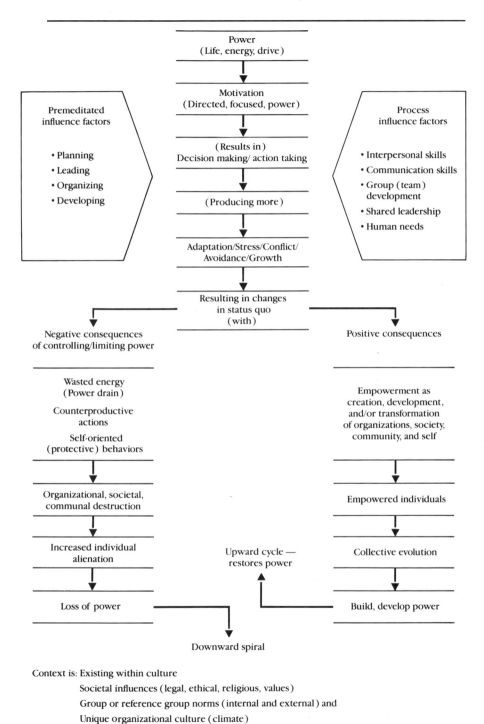

controlling organizational dynamic, awareness of that fact is the first step toward changing the zero-sum power drain. If the organization is capable of producing power based on how it is managed, the premeditated influence factors, and how people interact with each other, then the organization is already to some degree empowering.

Another way to facilitate self-awareness in organization-specific terms is to use management-style surveys such as those presented in the Appendix. They are designed to provide information on how managers see themselves in terms of the empowerment process, how those who work with them see them, and how the organization's culture relates to the empowerment issue.

Every activity inside and outside an organization sets up a dynamic chain of interactive relationships that is often difficult to see. Within this dynamic chain, an organization is created with the potential to empower or alienate.

The authors hope that the discussions in this book will help readers recognize which factors in their behavior and in the environment produce a positive empowerment process and which deny the creation of power. If enough individuals in the organization choose to take the empowerment path, it will become the path of the organization itself.

Change as an Evolutionary Process

To move along the empowerment path is to commit individuals and organizations to a process of learning. To date, the empowerment path has been the road less often taken. Attempting to move an organization along that path is to take a challenging, unpredictable journey in company with like-minded travelers. In its way, this journey is an expedition into the American way of life; it is guided by the United States Constitution and over two hundred years of striving for a new vision of how people can live and work together. The empowerment expedition is also an evolutionary journey that seeks a personal as well as an organizational transformation by tapping into the human potential for growth and development.

The empowerment concept is the first step on a journey that will offer countless opportunities to understand power in a completely new way. It alters a lifetime of thinking and the behaviors associated with that thinking and it conceives of the possibility of creating with others more power and more powerful organizations.

Most of all it offers a choice. Organizations are as yet in the earliest stages of this evolution but each new success at creating power helps establish the path for others to follow. The journey is a challenging one and has a potential for excitement and frustration. Like all journeys, it starts with a first step. The authors hope that the ideas explored in this book have empowered the reader to choose that new first step — and many more steps — to creating better and more humane organizations. We not only need these new, empowering organizations; we deserve them.

REFERENCES AND BIBLIOGRAPHY

Allaire, Y., & Firsirotu, M. (1985). How to implement radical change strategies in large organizations. *Sloan Management Review, 26*(3), 19–34.

Argyris, C. (1955). Top management dilemma: Company needs vs. individual development. *Personnel, 32*(2), 123–134.

Argyris, C. (1957). *Personality and organization: The conflict between system and the individual.* New York: Harper & Row.

Argyris, C. (1965). *Organization and innovation.* Homewood, IL: Richard D. Irwin.

Argyris, C. (1982). *Reasoning, learning, and action: Individual and organizational.* San Francisco: Jossey-Bass.

Bandura, A. (1977). Self-efficacy: Toward a theory of behavioral change. *Psychology Review, 84*(2), 191–225.

Bard, R., Bell, C., Stephen, L., & Webster, L. (1987). *The trainer's professional development handbook.* San Francisco: Jossey-Bass.

Barnard, C. (1968). *The functions of the executive.* Cambridge, MA: Harvard University Press.

Barnett, E. H. (1981). The development of personal power for women: An exploration of the process of empowerment. *Dissertation Abstracts International, 41,* 4522A–5271A (University Microfilms No. 8112232, 349).

Beckhard, R. (1966). An organization improvement program in a decentralized organization. *Journal of Applied Behavioral Science, 2*(1), 3–25.

Beer, M. (1980). *Organization change and development: A systems view.* Santa Monica, CA: Goodyear Publishing.

Bennis, W. G. (1966). *Changing organizations: Essays on the development of human interaction.* New York: McGraw-Hill.

Bennis, W. G. (1970). The change agents. In R. Golembiewski & A. Blumberg (Eds.), *Sensitivity and the laboratory approach.* Itasca, IL: F. E. Peacock.

Bennis, W. G. (1982a). The artform of leadership. *Training and Development Journal, 36*(4), 44–46.

Bennis, W. G. (1982b). Leadership transforms vision into action. *Industry Week, 213*(5), 54–56.

Bennis, W. G., Benne, K. D., & Chin, R. (Eds.). (1961). *The planning of change.* New York: Holt, Rinehart & Winston.

Bennis, W. G., Benne, K. D., Chin, R., & Corey, K. E. (Eds.). (1976). *The planning of change* (3rd ed.). New York: Holt, Rinehart & Winston.

Bennis, W. G., & Nanus, B. (1985). *Leaders: The strategies for taking charge.* New York: Harper & Row.

Bennis, W. G., Schein, E. H., Steele, F. I., & Berlew, D. E. (Eds.). (1964). *Interpersonal dynamics: Essays and readings on human interaction.* Homewood, IL: Dorsey Press.

Berger, P. L., & Neuhaus, R. J. (1977). *To empower people: The role of mediating structures in public policy.* Washington, DC: American Enterprise Institute for Public Policy Research.

Bernstein, P. (1976). *Workplace democratization: Its internal dynamics.* Unpublished manuscript, Kent State University, Kent, OH.

Block, P. (1987). *The empowered man-*

ager: Positive political skills at work. San Francisco: Jossey-Bass.

Bradford, D., & Cohen, A. R. (1984). *Managing for excellence: The guide to developing high performance in contemporary organizations.* New York: John Wiley.

Bradford, L. P., Gibb, J. R., & Benne, K. D. (Eds.). (1964). *T-group theory and laboratory method: Innovation in re-education.* New York: John Wiley.

Brinkerhoff, D. (1979). Inside public bureaucracy: Empowering managers to empower clients. *Rural Development Participation Review, 1*(1), 7–8.

Bryant, C., & White, L. G. (1982). *Managing development in the third world.* Boulder, CO: Westview Press.

Burns, J. M. (1978). *Leadership.* New York: Harper & Row.

Cartwright, D., & Zander, A. (Eds.). (1960). *Group dynamics: Research and theory* (2nd ed.). New York: Harper & Row.

Cheifetz, D. (1976). Giving children experience in power. *Learning, 4*(7).

Clark, J. V. (1962). Some troublesome dichotomies in human relations training. *Human Relations Training News, 6*(1), 3–6.

Combs, A. (1964). Helping young people discover commitment. *Educational Leadership, 22*(3), 164–169.

Connelly, S. L. (1988). *Work spirit.* Los Angeles: Work Spirit and Leadership.

Cooperrider, D. L. (1986). *The management of ideas: Empowering our methodology to create the future.* Unpublished manuscript.

Davis, S. A. (1967). An organic problem-solving method of organizational change. *Journal of Applied Behavioral Science, 3*(1), 3–21.

Dickson, P. (1984). *Conflict and power.* Unpublished manuscript, The University of West Florida, Pensacola.

Donnelly, J. H., Gibson, J. L., & Ivancevich, J. M. (1975). *Fundamentals of management: Functions, behaviors, models* (rev. ed.). Dallas, TX: Business Publications.

Elden, M., & Taylor, J. C. (1983). Participatory research at work: An introduction. *Journal of Occupational Behavior, 4*(1), 1–8.

Fainstein, M. I., & Martin, M. (1978). Support for community control among local urban elites. *Urban Affairs Quarterly, 13*(4), 443–465.

Fox, S. (1982, Nov. 21). What makes a superleader? Associated Press news release. (Interview conducted in Los Angeles.)

French, J. R. P., & Raven, B. (1960). The bases of social power. In D. Cartwright and A. F. Zander (Eds.), *Group dynamics: Research and theory* (2nd ed., pp. 607–623). New York: Harper & Row.

French, W. L., Kast, F. E., & Rosenzweig, J. E. (1985). *Understanding human behavior in organizations.* New York: Harper & Row.

Galbraith, J. (1977). *Organization design.* Reading, MA: Addison-Wesley.

Gibb, J. R. (1964). Climate for trust formation. In L. P. Bradford, J. R. Gibb, & K. D. Benne (Eds.), *T-group theory and laboratory method: Innovation in re-education,* New York: John Wiley.

Gibb, J. R. (1978). *Trust: A new view of personal & organizational development.* Cardiff, CA: Omicron Press.

Goffman, E. (1955). On face-work. *Psychiatry, 18*(3).

Golembiewski, R. T., & Blumberg, A. (Eds.). (1973). *Sensitivity training and the laboratory approach.* Itasca, IL: F. E. Peacock.

Greenfield, P. W. (Ed.). (1969). *The trust theory of group development.* Midland, MI: Dow Chemical Company.

Hampden-Turner, C. H. (1981). *Maps of the mind.* New York: Macmillan.

Harris, P. (1980). Innovating with high achievers in HRD. *Training and Development Journal, 34*(10), 45–50.

Harris, P. R., & Moran, R. T. (1987). *Managing cultural differences* (2nd ed.). Houston, TX: Gulf.

Harvey, J. B. (1974). The Abilene paradox: The management of agreement. *Organizational Dynamics, 3*(1), 63–80.

Hertzberg, F., Mausner, B., & Synderman, B. (1959). *Motivation to work.* New York: John Wiley.

Hoffman, C. (1978). Empowerment movements and mental health: Locus of control and commitment to the United Farm Workers. *Journal of Community Psychology, 6*(3), 216–221.

Hummel, R. P. (1982). *The bureaucratic experience* (2nd ed.). New York: St. Martin's Press.

Janis, I. L. (1972). *Victims of groupthink: A psychological study of foreign-pol-*

icy decisions and fiascoes. Boston: Houghton Mifflin.

Joiner, C. W., Jr. (1985). Making the 'Z' concept work. *Sloan Management Review, 26*(3), 57–63.

Kanter, R. M. (1977). *Men and women of the corporation.* New York: Basic Books.

Kanter, R. M. (1979). Power failure in management circuits. *Harvard Business Review, 57*(4), 65–75.

Kanter, R. M. (1983). *The change masters: Innovation for productivity in American culture.* New York: Simon & Schuster.

Kanter, R. M. (1987). Power in organizations. In D. W. Organ (Ed.), *The applied psychology of work behavior* (3rd ed., pp. 273–310). Plano, TX: Business Publications.

Kieffer, C. H. (1984). Citizen empowerment: A developmental perspective. *Prevention in Human Services, 213*(3), 9–36.

Knowles, M. S. (1975). *Self-directed learning: A guide for learners & teachers.* New York: Cambridge Books. .

Kolb, D., Rubin, I., & McIntyre, J. (1971). *Organizational psychology.* Englewood Cliffs, NJ: Prentice-Hall.

Kuttner, R. (1985). Sharing power at Eastern Airlines. *Harvard Business Review, 63*(6), 91–101.

Lederer, W. J., & Burdick, E. (1958). *The ugly American.* New York: W. W. Norton.

Lewin, K. (1947). Frontiers in group dynamics: Concept, method, and reality in social science. Social equilibria and social change. *Human Relations, 1*(1), 5–42.

Likert, R. (1967). *The human organization: Its management and value.* New York: McGraw-Hill.

Lippitt, G. L. (1966). Managing change: Six ways to turn resistance into acceptance. *Supervisory Management, 11*(8), 21–24.

Lippitt, G. L., & Lippitt, R. (1978). *The consulting process in action.* San Diego, CA: University Associates.

Lippitt, G. L., & This, L. E. (1967, March). Leaders for laboratory training: Selected guidelines for group trainers utilizing the laboratory method. *Training and Development Journal.*

Lippitt, R., & White, R. K. (1958). An experimental study of leadership and group life. In E. E. Maccoby, T. M. Newcomb, & E. L. Hartley (Eds.), *Readings in social psychology* (3rd ed., pp. 496–511). New York: Holt, Rinehart & Winston.

Liversidge, A. (1985). Mega-author John Naisbitt looks past the next trend. *Success Magazine.*

Loughary, J. W., & Ripley, T. (1977). *Self-empowerment.* Unpublished manuscript.

Loughary, J. W., & Ripley, T. (1982). *Career and life planning guide.* Aurora, IL: Caroline House.

Maccoby, M. (1977). *The gamesman: The new corporate leaders.* New York: Simon & Schuster.

Marrow, A. J., Bowers, D. G., & Seashore, S. E. (1967). *Management by participation: Creating a climate for person-*

al and organizational development. New York: Harper & Row.

Marsenich, B. (1983). How to teach the steps of change. *Training: The Magazine of Human Resources Development,* 62–63.

May, G. D., & Kruger, M. I. (1988). The manager within. *Personnel Journal, 67*(2), 56–65.

McCaby, M. (1981). *The leaders.* New York: Simon & Schuster.

McClelland, D. (1970). The two faces of power. *Journal of International Affairs, 24*(1), 29–47.

McClelland, D. (1975). *Power: The inner experience.* New York: Irvington/Halsted Press.

McClelland, D., Davis, W., Kalin, R., & Wanner, E. (1971). *The drinking man.* New York: Free Press.

McCluskey, J. E. (1976). Beyond the carrot and the stick: Liberation and power without control. In W. G. Bennis, K. D. Benne, & R. Chin (Eds.), *The planning of change* (3rd ed., pp. 382–403). New York: Holt, Rinehart & Winston.

McGregor, D. (1960). *The human side of enterprise.* New York: McGraw-Hill.

McGregor, D. (1967). *The professional manager.* New York: McGraw-Hill.

Mintzberg, H. (1983). *Power in and around organizations.* Englewood Cliffs, NJ: Prentice-Hall.

Moglen, H. (1983). Power and empowerment. *Women's Studies International Forum, 6*(2), 131–134.

Murrell, K. L. (1976a). *The General Foods multi-perspectual case study.* Unpublished manuscript, George

Washington University, Washington, DC.

Murrell, K. L. (1976b). *The I.G.P. multiperspectual case study.* Unpublished manuscript, George Washington University, Washington, DC.

Murrell, K. L. (1977). *An exploratory descriptive study of the relationship of alternative work organizations and quality of life: More modern times.* Unpublished doctoral dissertation, George Washington University, Washington, DC.

Murrell, K. L. (1984a). *The definition, the literature, and the initial conceptual underpinning of empowerment.* Unpublished manuscript, University of West Florida, Pensacola.

Murrell, K. L. (1984b). Organization development and the third world. *Organization Development Journal.*

Murrell, K. L. (1985). The development of a theory of empowerment: Rethinking power for organization development. *Organization Development Journal, 3*(2), 34–38.

Naisbitt, J. (1984). *Megatrends: Ten new directions transforming our lives.* New York: Warner Books.

National Training Laboratories. (1968). *Report.* Washington, DC.

O'Connell, B. (1978). From service to advocacy to empowerment. *Social Casework, 59*(4), 195–202.

Ouchi, W. G. (1981). *Theory Z: How American business can meet the Japanese challenge.* Reading, MA: Addison-Wesley.

Peck, M. S. (1978). *The road less trav-*

eled: A psychology of love, traditional values, and spiritual growth. New York: Simon & Schuster.

Perlman, J. (1979). Grassroots empowerment and government response. *Social Policy, 10*(2), 16–21.

Perry, H. L. (1980). The socioeconomic impact of black political empowerment in a rural southern locality. *Rural Sociology, 45*(2), 207–222.

Peters, T., & Waterman, R. (1982). *In search of excellence: Lessons from America's best-run companies.* New York: Harper & Row.

Rappaport, J. (1981). In praise of paradox: A social policy of empowerment over prevention. *American Journal of Community Psychology, 9*(1), 1–25.

Robertson, D. B. (Ed.). (1978). *Power and empowerment in higher education: Studies in honor of Louis Smith.* Lexington, KY: University Press of Kentucky.

Rogers, C. R. (1961). *On becoming a person: A therapist's view of psychotherapy.* Boston: Houghton Mifflin.

Rogers, C. R. (1967). A plan for self-directed change in an educational system. *Educational Leadership, 24*(8), 717–731.

Rogers, C. R. (1969). *Freedom to learn.* Columbus, OH: Charles Merrill.

Rogers, C. R. (1970). *Carl Rogers on encounter groups.* New York: Harper & Row.

Rogers, C. R. (1983). *Freedom to learn for the eighties.* Westerville, OH: Charles E. Merrill.

Rogers, E. M., & Larson, J. K. (1984). *Silicon Valley fever: Growth of high-technology culture.* New York: Basic Books.

Rubinstein, R. (1986). Reflections on action anthropology: Some developmental dynamics of an anthropological tradition. *Human Organization, 45*(3), 270–279.

Ruma, S. J. (1974). Social change — ideas and application: A diagnostic model for organizational change. *NTL Institute Report, 4*(4), 16.

Russel, B. (1983). *Power: A new social analysis.* London: G. Allen & Unwin.

Sampson, R. V. (1966). *The psychology of power.* New York: Pantheon Books.

Schaef, A. W., & Fassel, D. (1988). *The addictive organization.* New York: Harper & Row.

Schein, E. H. (1981). Improving face-to-face relationships. *Sloan Management Review, 22*(2), 43–52.

Schein, E. H., & Bennis, W. G. (Eds.). (1965). *Personal and organizational change through group methods: The laboratory approach.* New York: John Wiley.

Scott Paper Company (1987). Exploring the Scott vision.

Sheehy, G. (1976). *Passages: Predictable crises of adult life.* New York: E. P. Dutton.

Solomon, B. B. (1976). Black empowerment: Social work in oppressed communities. New York: Columbia University Press.

Srivastva, S., and Associates. (1986). *Executive power.* San Francisco: Jossey-Bass.

Stensrud, R. H., & Stensrud, K. (1982). Counseling for health empowerment. *Personnel and Guidance Journal, 60*(6), 377–380.

Swanson, G. E. (1973). The search for a guardian spirit: A process of empowerment in simpler societies. *Ethnology, 12*(3), 359–375.

Tannenbaum, R., Kallajian, V., & Weschler, I. R. (1954). Training managers for leadership. *Personnel, 30,* 3–11.

Taylor, L., with Falkner, D. (1987). *LT: Living on the edge.* New York: Times Books.

Thayer, F. C. (1981). *An end to hierarchy and competition: Administration in the post-affluent world* (2nd ed.). New York: New Viewpoints.

Thomas, K. W., & Velthouse, B. A. (1985). *Cognitive elements of empowerment.* Unpublished manuscript, University of Pittsburgh.

Thomas, K. W., & Velthouse, B. A. (1985, August). *Cognitive elements of empowerment.* Paper presented at the meeting of the Academy of Management, Los Angeles, CA.

Toffler, A. (1970). *Future shock.* New York: Bantam Books.

Toffler, A. (1980). *The third wave.* New York: Morrow.

Torbert, W. R. (1987). *Managing the corporate dream: Restructuring for long-term success.* Homewood, IL: Dow Jones-Irwin.

Truax, C. B. (1961). The process of group psychotherapy. *Psychological Monographs, 75*(7).

Vaill, P. B. (1982). The purpose of high performing systems. *Organizational Dynamics, 11*(2), 23–39.

Velthouse, B. A., & Thomas, K. W. (1985). *Empowerment, self-efficacy and behavior.* Unpublished manuscript, University of Pittsburgh.

Vogt, J., Cox, J. L., Velthouse, B. A., & Thames, B. H. (1983). *Retaining professional nurses: A planned process.* St. Louis: C. V. Mosby.

Vogt, J. F., & Holler, J. (1988). A readiness framework for changing traditional organizations to the all-salaried structure of the future, with a case study from industry. *Proceedings of the Southern Management Association,* Atlanta, GA.

Vogt, J. F., & Hunt, B. (1988). Not why, what really goes wrong with quality circles and other working groups. *Training and Development Journal, 42*(5), 96–100.

Walker, W., & Murrell, K. L. (1988). *Black empowerment in corporate America.* Unpublished working paper, University of West Florida, Pensacola.

Walton, R. (1985). From control to commitment in the workplace. *Harvard Business Review, 63*(2), 77–84.

Whyte, W. H. *The organization man.* (1956). New York: Simon & Schuster.

Yankelovich, D. (1981). *New rules: Searching for self-fulfillment in a world turned upside down.* New York: Random House.

APPENDIX

MANAGEMENT STYLES SURVEY: ORGANIZATIONAL CULTURE

The following survey is designed to help form a view of your organization's culture as directly affected by the prevailing management style. There are no right or wrong responses; the best response is the one that most accurately describes your organization. The survey is primarily for research purposes; your name will not ever be attached to your comments.

Name of organization _____

Years and months employed at this organization _____

Please respond to each item as truthfully as you can based on your view of the managers' behavior and actions and *not* on your guesses about what might be the "right answer." This survey is primarily to help your organization better understand the managerial style being practiced.

Circle the letter that best corresponds to your organization in the setting described. The two endpoints on each continuum, *R* and *G* or *N* and *E*, are defined, while the three points between them are not. Circle the midpoint only if the typical behavior in the organization falls equally as often at either endpoint; circle *O* or *B* or *A* or *U,* depending on which endpoint more closely resembles your organization. As much as possible, try to determine where the organization most *often* fits between the two endpoints.

185

Example: In managing people, managers in this organization normally

R	O	Y	B	G

Carefully supervise them and allow them to do only work that managers are sure they can handle.				Give them lots of freedom and put emphasis on results, not on how to do the job.

Final Scores

Transfer your scores from the Scoring Instructions at the end of the survey.

Area 1. _____

Area 2. _____

Area 3. _____

Area 4. _____

Area 5. _____

Area 6. _____

Total _____

SURVEY 1.

---

1. In communicating with subordinates, managers in this organization normally

R	O	Y	B	G

Provide only the information that is absolutely needed to do the job.

Provide more information than is needed and try to help subordinates understand the larger picture.

2. When managers around here make a decision and take action, they

N	U	L	A	E

Are usually in agreement with others concerned; their actions are seen as part of a larger whole.

See themselves as solely responsible; exert power as necessary.

3. In planning work, managers here seem to prefer to

R	O	Y	B	G
Do it themselves first, then show the boss, then tell subordinates what to expect.				Work with others to develop a larger plan first, then share the planning activity with subordinates.

4. When evaluating subordinates, managers normally

N	U	L	A	E
Share evaluations and give subordinates a chance to respond.				Fill out the proper form and send a copy to Personnel, but try not to make a big deal of it.

5. As leaders, managers always try to

R	O	Y	B	G
Be out in front of their subordinates and know more about the job than their employees do so they can lead.				Inspire others, set an example, work collaboratively with others.

6. In selecting people as new employees, managers here

N	U	L	A	E

Try to match the job and person for long-term success.				Try to screen out trouble-makers, lazy people, and those they could not manage well.

7. In this organization the idea of a perfect information system is one that

N	U	L	A	E

Gives as many people as possible access to nonconfidential information.				Provides others with *only* the information they need to do the present job.

8. When pressure is on for a fast decision, managers in this organization

R	O	Y	B	G

Immediately make a decision and take responsibility for it.				Quickly size up the situation; determine whether anyone else needs to be involved; and, if so, delay making a decision.

9. When organizing work and subordinates, managers here

N	U	L	A	E
Carefully explain the larger picture and then work with the groups involved to define their responsibilities and power.				Clearly describe each person's job, responsibilities, and report structure.

10. The people who work for me always know

R	O	Y	B	G
I am boss and my evaluations will be very important to them for raises and promotions.				How they are doing, in what areas they are doing well, and in what areas they need improvement.

11. When I try to motivate my employees, I

N	U	L	A	E
Look for the kind of work and setting in which they can perform best.				Give them rewards and punishment as appropriate.

12. When an individual does not perform a job well, I usually

R	O	Y	B	G

Counsel the person and, if that does not work, look for a replacement before terminating that person.				Sit down with the person and try to determine what it will take to get the job done well.

13. In talking about my job with people I work with, I try to

R	O	Y	B	G

Tell them only what I think they have a right to know.				Discuss my work freely in hopes that they might be able to assist me or that I might be able to help them.

14. When it comes to action, I am firmly convinced that

N	U	L	A	E
The power of the group to decide and act should prevail if the conditions are right and the group has reached an advanced stage of development.				An individual can get much more done more quickly than any group.

15. To get a work project accomplished, managers here

R	O	Y	B	G
Tell their subordinates exactly what to do one step at a time, then tell them how much time they have to complete each step.				Coordinate the total project first, then go back over each step so that everyone knows what is required and how his or her work fits into the project as a whole.

16. In order to control the organization, managers

N	U	L	A	E
Help subordinates build self-control and establish higher levels of responsibility in the organization.				Keep a careful eye on all that goes on and make sure there is a developed system of controls.

17. Managers here act as if the best rewards for people are

R	O	Y	B	G
More money, more time off, and more status.				Recognition and satisfaction resulting from doing a good job.

18. When working with people, managers act as if

N	U	L	A	E
Workers can always achieve more; together they can make any situation better; they can learn from working together.				Workers will be rewarded when they do as they are told; if they do not, they will be disciplined.

19. When managers communicate with their bosses or those in higher positions, they are

N	U	L	A	E

Eager to explain what they know and think about any subject that seems important.				Very cautious of what they say lest they give the wrong impression or tell too much.

20. When a manager's boss delegates a job, the subordinate manager will usually

R	O	Y	B	G

Take full responsibility and get the job done by himself or herself whenever possible.				Work with others in getting the job done and in ensuring and sharing success.

21. When a work project is very complicated and involved, managers in this organization prefer to

N	U	L	A	E
Work with a team to ensure that all the pieces fit together and that everyone knows what everyone else is doing.				Take complete charge and simplify each part so they can manage it rather than depending on people's ability to work together.

22. Managers here act as if the best way to be sure work is done on time is to

R	O	Y	B	G
Set specific deadlines, constantly monitor progress, and discipline those who are late.				Be sure everyone understands the deadlines and how they affect others' work; reward and recognize timely performance.

23. In leadership I think it is most important to

N	U	L	A	E
Work with people in such a way that they become more powerful and able to be successful.				Always show that you know where you are going and have strength and confidence in your own opinions.

24. If I have worked with people for several years, I

R	O	Y	B	G
Feel they should know their jobs and what is expected of them.				Should be able to see how much they have grown in their jobs and how much more valuable they are to the organization.

25. When I receive information, I usually

G	B	Y	O	R
Do whatever I can to ensure that information goes where it is needed to get the job done.				Make sure information is needed before passing it along.

26. I encourage my subordinates to

N	U	L	A	E

Work as part of a team, which is more powerful than individual members and able to do more without my help.				Work alone and report primarily to me because I will take care of them.

27. Managers assume that the best way to design an organization is to

R	O	Y	B	G

Centralize power and authority so that people on each step of the organization know all that is going on.				Encourage delegation of authority and power sharing as much as possible so as to use all employees fully.

28. When an employee needs to be disciplined, this organization's managers try to

N	U	L	A	E
Discuss the problem and look for longer-term solutions before punishment is given; document the infraction.				Make sure the punishment fits the "crime" and that everyone knows what happens to problem employees.

29. When managers work with unmotivated employees, they usually

R	O	Y	B	G
Try to figure out what it will take to make them work and watch them closely to keep them moving.				Work with them to figure out what is going on, then help them find the work best suited to their abilities or help them find another job.

30. If someone is not growing in his or her job, managers here usually

N	U	L	A	E

Try to
understand the
problem and
do whatever
they can to
help.

Feel there are
no problems as
long as the
person still gets
the work done
and works well
with the boss.

SCORING INSTRUCTIONS

For each of the following areas, add up the number of responses for each letter, and write that number in the appropriate space. Multiply that number by the figure shown, and add the result in order to find the total numerical score for that set of questions. Enter the final scores on page 186.

Area	Question	Letter circled	Number of responses			Total score of area
1: Information	1	_____	R, E _____	×	0 = _____	
communication	7	_____	O, A _____	×	2 = _____	
	13	_____	Y, L _____	×	5 = _____	
	19	_____	B, U _____	×	8 = _____	
	25	_____	G, N _____	×	10 = _____	_____
2: Decision making/	2	_____	R, E _____	×	0 = _____	
action	8	_____	O, A _____	×	2 = _____	
	14	_____	Y, L _____	×	5 = _____	
	20	_____	B, U _____	×	8 = _____	
	26	_____	G, N _____	×	10 = _____	_____
3: Planning/	3	_____	R, E _____	×	0 = _____	
organizing	9	_____	O, A _____	×	2 = _____	
	15	_____	Y, L _____	×	5 = _____	
	21	_____	B, U _____	×	8 = _____	
	27	_____	G, N _____	×	10 = _____	_____

Area	Question	Letter circled	Number of responses			Total score of area
4: Evaluating/control	4	_____	R, E _____	×	0 = _____	
	10	_____	O, A _____	×	2 = _____	
	16	_____	Y, L _____	×	5 = _____	
	22	_____	B, U _____	×	8 = _____	
	28	_____	G, N _____	×	10 = _____	_____
5: Leadership/ motivation	5	_____	R, E _____	×	0 = _____	
	11	_____	O, A _____	×	2 = _____	
	17	_____	Y, L _____	×	5 = _____	
	23	_____	B, U _____	×	8 = _____	
	29	_____	G, N _____	×	10 = _____	_____
6: Selection/ placement/ development	6	_____	R, E _____	×	0 = _____	
	12	_____	O, A _____	×	2 = _____	
	18	_____	Y, L _____	×	5 = _____	
	24	_____	B, U _____	×	8 = _____	
	30	_____	G, N _____	×	10 = _____	_____

Total score of all six areas _____

Placement of Scores

Area 1. Score + _____ : Management-information/communication-system skills

Area 2. Score + _____ : Decision-making and action-taking skills

Area 3. Score + _____ : Project-planning, organizing, and system-integration skills

Area 4. Score + _____ : Systems-evaluation and internal-control skills

Area 5. Score + _____ : Leadership, motivation, and reward-systems skills

Area 6. Score + _____ : Selection, placement, and development of people skills

Total _____ : Total for all managerial functions

For each area score, place an *X* on the area line at the location corresponding to your score.

SURVEY 1.   Area Scores

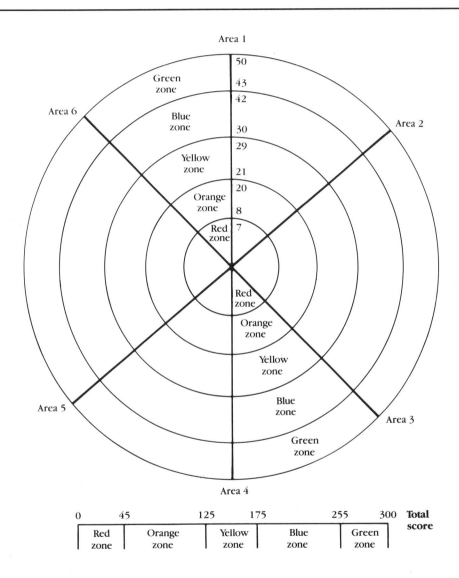

INTERPRETATION OF SCORES

◆ *Red Zone* = Area scores of 0–7, total scores of 0–45.

(R–E) Personalized Power Extreme Area. This area reflects the manager who tightly controls the power in the organization. He or she uses the least empowering style of management and is very concerned with control or power.

◆ *Orange Zone* = Area scores of 8–20, total scores of 46–125.

(O–A) Controlling Style. This zone reflects a managerial style that is more control oriented and less empowering or oriented toward sharing power. The manager is not extremely control oriented but seldom shares, creates, or empowers subordinates.

◆ *Yellow Zone* = Area scores of 21–29, total scores of 126–174.

(Y–L) Middle-Road Area. This middle-ground style combines the two styles of controlling and empowering in somewhat equal proportions. This position may reflect a person who rarely acts in the extreme in matters concerning the use of power.

◆ *Blue Zone* = Area scores of 30–42, total scores of 175–254.

(B–U) Empowerment Style. The manager in this zone uses a style that is more empowering than controlling.

◆ *Green Zone* = Area scores of 43–50, total scores of 255–300.

(G–N) Socialized Power Extreme Zone. This zone reflects the manager who shares power and employs the most empowering managerial style. This style not only shares power but also creates it.

MANAGEMENT-STYLES SURVEY: SUBORDINATES' PERCEPTIONS

The following survey is designed to help your manager understand how others perceive his or her management style. There are no right or wrong answers; the best answer is the one that most accurately describes your manager's behavior. The survey is primarily for your manager's own use; your name will not be attached to your comments.

Manager's name ——————————— **Job title** ———————————————

Please respond to each item as truthfully as you can based on your view of your manager's behavior and actions and *not* on your guesses about what might be the "right answer." This survey is primarily to help your manager better understand his or her managerial style.

  Circle the letter that best corresponds to your manager's behavior in the setting described. The two endpoints on each continuum, *R* and *G* or *N* and *E*, are defined, while the three points between them are not. Circle the midpoint only if your manager behaves equally as often at either endpoint; circle *O* or *B* or *A* or *U,* depending on which endpoint best describes his or her behavior. As much as possible, try to determine where your manager's behavior most *often* occurs between the two endpoints.

Example: In managing people, my manager normally

R	O	Y	B	G

Carefully supervises them and allows them to do only the work he or she is sure they can handle.				Gives them lots of freedom and puts the emphasis on results, not on how to do the job.

Final Scores

Transfer your scores from the Scoring Instructions at the end of the survey.

Area 1. _____

Area 2. _____

Area 3. _____

Area 4. _____

Area 5. _____

Area 6. _____

Total _____

SURVEY 2.

---

1. When communicating with subordinates, my manager normally

R	**O**	**Y**	**B**	**G**

Provides only the information that is absolutely needed to do the job.				Provides more information than is needed and tries to help subordinates understand the larger picture.

2. When my manager makes a decision and takes action, she or he

N	**U**	**L**	**A**	**E**

Is usually in agreement with others; his or her actions are seen as part of a larger whole.				Sees himself or herself as the sole person responsible; exerts power as necessary.

3. When planning, my manager prefers to

R	**O**	**Y**	**B**	**G**

Do it himself or herself first, then show the boss, then tell subordinates what to expect.				Work with others to develop a larger plan first, then share the planning activity with subordinates.

4. When evaluating subordinates, my manager normally

N	U	L	A	E
Shares evaluations and gives subordinates a chance to respond.				Fills out the proper forms and sends a copy to Personnel but tries not to make a big deal of it.

5. As a leader, my manager always tries to

R	O	Y	B	G
Be out in front of his or her people; maintain superior knowledge of employees' jobs to ensure his or her position of leadership.				Inspire others, set an example, and work collaboratively with others.

6. When selecting new employees, my manager

N	U	L	A	E
Tries to match the job to the person to facilitate long-term success.				Tries to screen out troublemakers, lazy people, and those he or she could not manage well.

7. My manager's idea of a perfect information system would

N	U	L	A	E

Give as many people as possible access to non-confidential information.				Provide others with *only* the information they need to do the present job.

8. When pressured to make a decision, my manager

R	O	Y	B	G

Immediately makes a decision and takes responsibility for it.				Quickly sizes up the situation; determines whether anyone else needs to be involved; and, if so, delays making a decision.

9. When organizing work and subordinates, my manager

N	U	L	A	E

Carefully explains the larger picture and then works with the groups involved to define their responsibilities and power.				Clearly describes each person's job, responsibilities, and reporting structure.

10. The people who work for my manager always know

R	O	Y	B	G

That he/she is the boss and that his/her evaluations will be very important to them for raises and promotions.				How they are doing, in what areas they are doing well, and in what areas they need improvement.

11. When trying to motivate employees, my manager

N	U	L	A	E

Looks for the kind of work and setting in which they can perform best.				Gives them rewards and punishment as appropriate.

12. When an individual does not perform a job well, my manager usually

R	O	Y	B	G

Counsels the person and, if that does not work, looks for a replacement before terminating that person.				Sits down with the person and tries to determine what it will take to get the job done well.

13. When discussing positions with employees, my manager tries to

R	O	Y	B	G

Tell them only what he or she thinks they have a right to know.				Discuss the work freely, encourage subordinates' suggestions and comments, and look for opportunities to help them.

14. My manager seems firmly convinced that when it comes to action,

N	U	L	A	E

The power of the group to decide and act should prevail if the conditions are right and the group is well developed.				An individual can get much more done more quickly than any group.

15. To get a work project accomplished, my manager

R	O	Y	B	G
Tells his or her subordinates exactly what to do one step at a time, then tells them how much time they have to complete each step.				Coordinates the total project first, then goes back over each step so that everyone knows what is required and how his or her work fits into the project as a whole.

16. My manager's approach to control is to

N	U	L	A	E
Help subordinates build self-control and achieve higher levels of responsibility in the organization.				Keep a careful eye on all that goes on and make sure there is a developed system of controls.

17. My manager seems to believe that employees are motivated by

R	O	Y	B	G

More money, more time off, and more status.				Recognition and satisfaction resulting from doing a good job.

18. When working with people, my manager acts as if

N	U	L	A	E

We can always achieve more; together any situation can be made better; we can learn from working together.				You will be rewarded if you do as you are told; if you do not, you will be disciplined.

19. When my manager communicates with his or her boss or those in higher positions, he or she is

N	U	L	A	E

Eager to explain his/her knowledge and opinions.				Very cautious of what he/she says lest he/she gives the wrong impression or tells too much.

20. When my manager's boss delegates a job to him/her, my manager will usually

R	O	Y	B	G

Take full responsibility and get the job done by himself or herself whenever possible.				Work with others in getting the job done, and in ensuring and sharing success.

21. When a work project is very complicated and involved, my manager prefers to

N	U	L	A	E

Work with a team to ensure that all the pieces fit together and that everyone knows what everyone else is doing.				Take complete charge and simplify each part so that the project is manageable, rather than depending on people's ability to work together.

22. My manager acts as if the best way to be sure work is done on time is to

R	O	Y	B	G
Set specific deadlines, constantly monitor progress, and discipline those who are late.				Be sure everyone understands the deadlines and how they affect others' work; reward and recognize timely performance.

23. According to my manager, leadership means

N	U	L	A	E
Working with people in such a way that they become more powerful and successful.				Demonstrating that you know where you are going and have strength and confidence in your own opinions.

24. If my manager worked with someone for several years, he or she

R	O	Y	B	G
Would know the boundaries of the job and the boss's expectations.				Should have a sense of growth in the job and of the person's increased value to the organization.

25. When communicating information, my manager usually

G	B	Y	O	R
Does whatever he or she can to ensure that information goes where it is needed to get the job done.				Makes sure information is needed before passing it along.

26. My manager encourages his or her subordinates to

N	U	L	A	E
Work together as a team because teams have more power and can accomplish more than the same number of individuals working alone.				Work alone and report primarily to the manager because the manager takes care of his or her subordinates.

27. My manager assumes that the best way to design an organization is to

R	O	Y	B	G

Centralize power and authority so that all employees are informed about managerial decisions and organizational happenings.				Encourage delegation of authority and power sharing as much as possible in order to use each employee to his or her performance capacity.

28. When an employee needs to be disciplined, my manager tries to

N	U	L	A	E

Discuss the problem, look for longer-term solutions before punishment is given, and document the infraction.				Make sure the punishment fits the "crime" and that everyone knows what happens to problem employees.

29. When my manager works with unmotivated employees, he or she usually

R	O	Y	B	G

Tries to figure out what it will take to make them work and watches them closely to keep them moving.

Works with them to figure out what is going on, then helps them find the work best suited to their abilities or helps them find another job.

30. If someone is not growing in his or her job, my manager usually

N	U	L	A	E

Tries to understand the problem and does whatever is possible to help.

Believes there are no problems as long as the person still gets the work done and works well with him or her.

SCORING INSTRUCTIONS

For each of the following areas, add up the number of responses for each letter, and write that number in the appropriate space. Multiply that number by the figure shown, and add the result in order to find the total numerical score for that set of questions. Enter the final scores on page 204.

Area	Question	Letter circled	Number of responses				Total score of area
1: Information communication	1	_____	R, E _____	×	0	= _____	
	7	_____	O, A _____	×	2	= _____	
	13	_____	Y, L _____	×	5	= _____	
	19	_____	B, U _____	×	8	= _____	
	25	_____	G, N _____	×	10	= _____	_____
2: Decision making/ action	2	_____	R, E _____	×	0	= _____	
	8	_____	O, A _____	×	2	= _____	
	14	_____	Y, L _____	×	5	= _____	
	20	_____	B, U _____	×	8	= _____	
	26	_____	G, N _____	×	10	= _____	_____
3: Planning/ organizing	3	_____	R, E _____	×	0	= _____	
	9	_____	O, A _____	×	2	= _____	
	15	_____	Y, L _____	×	5	= _____	
	21	_____	B, U _____	×	8	= _____	
	27	_____	G, N _____	×	10	= _____	_____
4: Evaluating/control	4	_____	R, E _____	×	0	= _____	
	10	_____	O, A _____	×	2	= _____	
	16	_____	Y, L _____	×	5	= _____	
	22	_____	B, U _____	×	8	= _____	
	28	_____	G, N _____	×	10	= _____	_____
5: Leadership/ motivation	5	_____	R, E _____	×	0	= _____	
	11	_____	O, A _____	×	2	= _____	
	17	_____	Y, L _____	×	5	= _____	
	23	_____	B, U _____	×	8	= _____	
	29	_____	G, N _____	×	10	= _____	_____
6: Selection/ placement/ development	6	_____	R, E _____	×	0	= _____	
	12	_____	O, A _____	×	2	= _____	
	18	_____	Y, L _____	×	5	= _____	
	24	_____	B, U _____	×	8	= _____	
	30	_____	G, N _____	×	10	= _____	_____

Total score of all six areas _____

Placement of Scores

Area 1. Score + _____ : Management-information/communication-system skills

Area 2. Score + _____ : Decision-making and action-taking skills

Area 3. Score + _____ : Project-planning, organizing, and system-integration skills

Area 4. Score + _____ : Systems-evaluation and internal-control skills

Area 5. Score + _____ : Leadership, motivation, and reward-systems skills

Area 6. Score + _____ : Selection, placement, and development of people skills

Total   _____ : Total for all managerial functions

For each area score, place an *X* on the area line at the location corresponding to your score.

SURVEY 2.   Area Scores

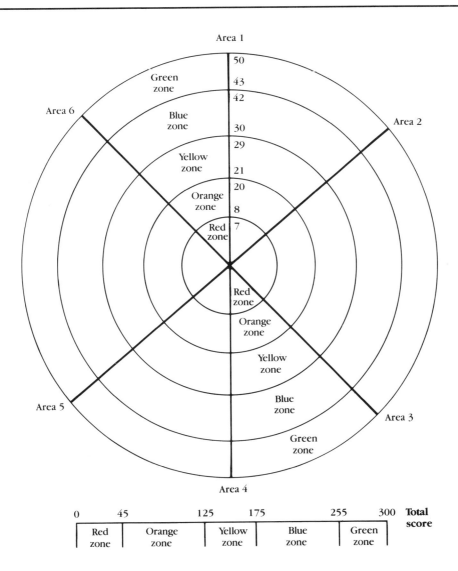

INTERPRETATION OF SCORES

◆ *Red Zone* = Area scores of 0–7, total scores of 0–45.
   (R–E) Personalized Power Extreme Area. This area reflects the manager
   who tightly controls the power in the organization. He or she uses the least

empowering style of management and is very concerned with control or power.

◆ *Orange Zone* = Area scores of 8–20, total scores of 46–125.

(O–A) Controlling Style. This zone reflects a managerial style that is more control oriented and less empowering or oriented toward sharing power. The manager is not extremely control oriented but seldom shares, creates, or empowers subordinates.

◆ *Yellow Zone* = Area scores of 21–29, total scores of 126–174.

(Y–L) Middle-Road Area. This middle-ground style combines the two styles of controlling and empowering in somewhat equal proportions. This position may reflect a person who rarely acts in the extreme in matters concerning the use of power.

◆ *Blue Zone* = Area scores of 30–42, total scores of 175–254.

(B–U) Empowerment Style. The manager in this zone uses a style that is more empowering than controlling.

◆ *Green Zone* = Area scores of 43–50, total scores of 255–300.

(G–N) Socialized Power Extreme Zone. This zone reflects the manager who shares power and employs the most empowering managerial style. This style not only shares power but also creates it.

MANAGEMENT-STYLES SURVEY: MANAGER'S PERCEPTION

The following survey is designed to help you identify and understand your own management style. There are no right or wrong answers; the best answer is the one that most accurately describes your own behavior. The survey is primarily for your own use; your name will not be attached to your results. We would, however, like to compare your responses with those of others. This survey will be most useful if your answers are as candid as possible. Your answers to the following questions will be used for data-comparison purposes.

Education level _____ Degree area _____

Age _____ Sex _____ Race _____ Citizenship _____

Occupation _____ Job Title _____

Please respond to each item as truthfully as you can based on your view of your behavior and actions and *not* on your guesses about what might be the "right answer." Again, this survey is primarily to help you better understand your own managerial style.

Circle the letter that best corresponds to your own behavior in the setting described. The two endpoints on each continuum, *R* and *G* or *N* and *E*, are defined, while the three points between them are not. Circle the midpoint only if you behave equally as often at either endpoint; circle *O* or *B* or *A* or *U*, depending on which endpoint best describes your behavior. As much as possible, try to determine where your behavior most *often* occurs between the two endpoints.

Example: In managing people, I normally

R	O	Y	B	G

Carefully supervise them and allow them to do only the work I am sure they can handle.	Give them lots of freedom and put the emphasis on results, not how to do the job.

Final Scores

Transfer your scores from the Scoring Instructions at the end of the question-naire.

Area 1. _____

Area 2. _____

Area 3. _____

Area 4. _____

Area 5. _____

Area 6. _____

Total _____

SURVEY 3.

---

1. When communicating with my subordinates, I normally

R	O	Y	B	G

R	O	Y	B	G
Provide only the information that is absolutely needed to do the job.				Provide more information than is needed and try to help them understand the larger picture.

2. When I make a decision and take action, I am

N	U	L	A	E

N	U	L	A	E
Usually in agreement with the others concerned; my actions are seen as part of a larger whole.				The sole person responsible; I exert my power as necessary.

3. When planning, I prefer to

R	O	Y	B	G

R	O	Y	B	G
Do it myself first, then show my boss, then tell my subordinates what to expect.				Work with others to develop a larger plan first, then share the planning activity with my subordinates.

4. When evaluating my subordinates, I normally

N	U	L	A	E
Share my evaluations and give subordinates a chance to respond.				Fill out the proper forms and send a copy to Personnel but try not to make a big deal of it.

5. As a leader, I always try to

R	O	Y	B	G
Be out in front of my people; know more about their jobs than they do in order to preserve my leadership status.				Inspire others, set an example, and work collaboratively with others.

6. When selecting new employees, I

N	U	L	A	E
Try to match the job to the person to facilitate long-term success.				Try to screen out troublemakers, lazy people, and those I could not manage well.

7. If I could build the perfect information system, it would

N	U	L	A	E

Give as many people as possible access to non-confidential information.

Provide others with *only* the information they needed to get their jobs done.

8. When I am pressured for a fast decision, I

R	O	Y	B	G

Immediately make a decision and take responsibility for it.

Quickly size up the situation; determine whether anyone else needs to be involved, and, if so, delay making a decision.

9. When I organize my work and my subordinates, I

N	U	L	A	E
Carefully explain the larger picture and then work with the groups involved to define their responsibilities.				Clearly describe each person's job, responsibilities, and reporting structure.

10. The people who work for me always know

R	O	Y	B	G
I am the boss, and my evaluations of their performance will determine such things as raises and promotions.				How they are doing, in what areas they are doing well, and in what areas they need improvement.

11. To motivate employees, I

N	U	L	A	E
Look for the kind of work and the setting in which they can best perform.				Reward and punish them as I deem appropriate.

12. When a subordinate does not perform a job well, I usually

R	**O**	**Y**	**B**	**G**
Counsel that person and, if that does not work, look for a replacement before terminating that person.				Sit down with the person and try to determine what it will take to get the job done well.

13. When discussing my job with co-workers, I try to

R	**O**	**Y**	**B**	**G**
Reveal only what I think they have a right to know.				Discuss my work freely— perhaps they can assist me or I can help them.

14. When it comes to action, I am firmly convinced that

N	**U**	**L**	**A**	**E**
The power of the group to decide and act should prevail if the conditions are right and the group is well developed.				An individual can get much more done more quickly than any group.

15. To get a work project accomplished, it is best to

R	O	Y	B	G
Tell subordinates exactly what to do one step at a time, then tell them how much time they have to complete each step.				Coordinate the total project first, then go back over each step so that everyone knows what is required and how his or her work fits into the project as a whole.

16. My approach to control is to

N	U	L	A	E
Help subordinates build self-control and achieve higher levels of responsibility in the organization.				Keep a careful eye on all that goes on and be sure there is a developed system of controls.

17. In my experience, I have found that subordinates are most motivated by

R	O	Y	B	G
More money, more time off, and more status.				Recognition and satisfaction resulting from doing a good job.

18. When working with people I try to act as if

N	U	L	A	E

Employees can always achieve more; together we can make any situation better; we can learn from working together.

Employees will be rewarded when they do as they are told; if they do not, they will be disciplined.

19. When I communicate with my boss or those in higher positions, I am

N	U	L	A	E

Eager to explain what I know and what I think about any subject that seems important.

Very cautious of what I say lest I give the wrong impression or say too much.

20. When my boss delegates a job to me, I will usually

R	O	Y	B	G

Take full responsibility and get the job done by myself whenever possible.

Work with others to get the job done and to ensure and share success.

21. When a work project is very complicated and involved, my manager prefers to

N	U	L	A	E
Work with a team to ensure that all the pieces fit together and that everyone knows what everyone else is doing.				Take complete charge and simplify each part so that the project is manageable, rather than depending on people's ability to work together.

22. The best way to ensure that work is done on time is to

R	O	Y	B	G
Set specific deadlines, constantly monitor progress, and discipline those who are late.				Be sure everyone understands the deadlines and how they affect others' work; reward and recognize timely performance.

23. In leadership it is most important to

N	U	L	A	E
Work with people in such a way that they become more powerful and successful.				Always show that you know where you are going and have strength and confidence in your own opinions.

24. If I have worked with someone for several years, I

R	O	Y	B	G
Believe he or she should know the boundaries of the job and what I expect.				Should be able to see how he or she has grown in the job and become more valuable to the organization.

25. When communicating information, I usually

G	B	Y	O	R
Do whatever I can to ensure that information goes where it is needed to get the job done.				Make sure information is needed before passing it along.

26. I encourage my subordinates to

N	U	L	A	E

Work as a team; teams are more powerful than people working alone and are able to do more without my help.				Work alone and report to me because I will take care of them.

27. The best way to design an organization is to

R	O	Y	B	G

Centralize power and authority so that all employees are informed about managerial decisions and organizational happenings.				Encourage delegation of authority and power sharing as much as possible in order to use all employees to their capacities.

28. When an employee needs to be disciplined, I try to

N	U	L	A	E

| Discuss the problem, look for longer-term solutions before punishment is given, and document the infraction. | | | | Make sure the punishment fits the "crime" and let everyone know what happens to problem employees. |

29. When I work with unmotivated employees, I usually

R	O	Y	B	G

| Try to figure out what it will take to make them work and watch them closely to keep them moving. | | | | Work with them to get to know them better, then help them find the work best suited to their abilities or help them find another job. |

30. If someone is not growing in his or her job, I usually

N	U	L	A	E

| Try to understand the problem and do whatever I can to help. | | | | Believe there are no problems as long as the person still gets the work done and works well with his or her boss. |

SCORING INSTRUCTIONS

For each of the following areas, add up the number of responses for each letter, and write that number in the appropriate space. Multiply that number by the figure shown, and add the result in order to find the total numerical score for that set of questions. Enter the final scores on page 222.

Area	Question	Letter circled	Number of responses			Total score of area
1: Information	1	_____	R, E _____	×	0 = _____	
communication	7	_____	O, A _____	×	2 = _____	
	13	_____	Y, L _____	×	5 = _____	
	19	_____	B, U _____	×	8 = _____	
	25	_____	G, N _____	×	10 = _____	_____
2: Decision making/	2	_____	R, E _____	×	0 = _____	
action	8	_____	O, A _____	×	2 = _____	
	14	_____	Y, L _____	×	5 = _____	
	20	_____	B, U _____	×	8 = _____	
	26	_____	G, N _____	×	10 = _____	_____

Area	Question	Letter circled	Number of responses			Total score of area
3: Planning/	3	_____	R, E _____	×	0 = _____	
organizing	9	_____	O, A _____	×	2 = _____	
	15	_____	Y, L _____	×	5 = _____	
	21	_____	B, U _____	×	8 = _____	
	27	_____	G, N _____	×	10 = _____	_____
4: Evaluating/control	4	_____	R, E _____	×	0 = _____	
	10	_____	O, A _____	×	2 = _____	
	16	_____	Y, L _____	×	5 = _____	
	22	_____	B, U _____	×	8 = _____	
	28	_____	G, N _____	×	10 = _____	_____
5: Leadership/	5	_____	R, E _____	×	0 = _____	
motivation	11	_____	O, A _____	×	2 = _____	
	17	_____	Y, L _____	×	5 = _____	
	23	_____	B, U _____	×	8 = _____	
	29	_____	G, N _____	×	10 = _____	_____
6: Selection/	6	_____	R, E _____	×	0 = _____	
placement/	12	_____	O, A _____	×	2 = _____	
development	18	_____	Y, L _____	×	5 = _____	
	24	_____	B, U _____	×	8 = _____	
	30	_____	G, N _____	×	10 = _____	_____

Total score of all six areas _____

Placement of Scores

Area 1. Score + _____ : Management-information/communication-system skills

Area 2. Score + _____ : Decision-making and action-taking skills

Area 3. Score + _____ : Project-planning, organizing, and system-integration skills

Area 4. Score + _____ : Systems-evaluation and internal-control skills

Area 5. Score + _____ : Leadership, motivation, and reward-systems skills

Area 6. Score + _____ : Selection, placement, and development of people skills

Total _____ : Total for all managerial functions

For each area score, place an *X* on the area line at the location corresponding to your score.

SURVEY 3. Area Scores

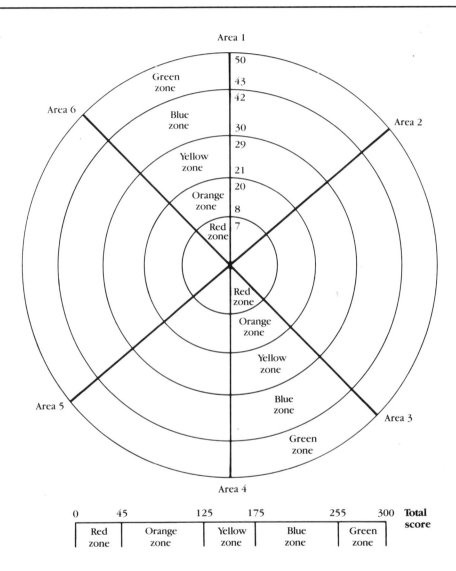

Area 1

Green
zone

50

43

42

Blue
zone

30

29

Yellow
zone

21

20

Orange
zone

8

Red 7
zone

Area 6

Area 2

Red
zone

Orange
zone

Yellow
zone

Blue
zone

Area 5

Area 3

Green
zone

Area 4

0	45	125	175	255	300	**Total**
Red zone	Orange zone	Yellow zone	Blue zone	Green zone		**score**

INTERPRETATION OF SCORES

◆ *Red Zone* = Area scores of 0–7, total scores of 0–45.

(R–E) Personalized Power Extreme Area. This area reflects the manager who tightly controls the power in the organization. He or she uses the least

empowering style of management and is very concerned with control or power.

♦ *Orange Zone* = Area scores of 8–20, total scores of 46–125.

(O–A) Controlling Style. This zone reflects a managerial style that is more control oriented and less empowering or oriented toward sharing of power. The manager is not extremely control oriented but seldom shares, creates, or empowers subordinates.

♦ *Yellow Zone* = Area scores of 21–29, total scores of 126–174.

(Y–L) Middle-Road Area. This middle-ground style combines the two styles of controlling and empowering in somewhat equal proportions. This position may reflect a person who rarely acts in the extreme in matters concerning the use of power.

♦ *Blue Zone* = Area scores of 30–42, total scores of 175–254.

(B–U) Empowerment Style. The manager in this zone uses a style that is more empowering than controlling.

♦ *Green Zone* = Area scores of 43–50, total scores of 255–300.

(G–N) Socialized Power Extreme Zone. This zone reflects the manager who shares power and employs the most empowering managerial style. This style not only shares power but also creates it.

INDEX